T0299242

Understanding the Born Global Firm

'Neri Karra's personal and in-depth exposition of fascinating enterprise is highly compelling. The treatment of the birth and growth of this enterprise is explained analytically, and with the use of theoretical constructs. A must read for any student of the international enterprise. The writing style is engaging and informative.'

S. Tamer Cavusgil, Callaway Professorial Chair, Georgia State University, Atlanta, USA

The challenges and opportunities that are presented to both small- and medium-sized enterprises have changed dramatically in recent decades as the world's economy becomes more globalized. The policies of open borders, a decrease in protectionism, and the demise of the nation-state have enabled small and large firms to engage in international activity from the outset.

Understanding the Born Global Firm combines the many different theoretical perspectives on born globals that have been previously researched, providing a unified framework to connect the antecedents, types, and outcomes of entrepreneurial activities pursued by such new ventures. A central case study of an international fashion firm which operates in over nine countries runs through the text, highlighting the formation and success of born globals and the importance of cultural competence.

This book will be invaluable to postgraduate students in the field of international business, entrepreneurship, ethnic entrepreneurs, global entrepreneurship, and international networks.

Neri Karra is an Associate Professor of Strategy and Entrepreneurship at IESEG School of Management based in Paris, France. She is also the founder of the Neri Karra luxury fashion brand.

Routledge Focus on Business and Management

The fields of business and management have grown exponentially as areas of research and education. This growth presents challenges for readers trying to keep up with the latest important insights. Routledge Focus on Business and Management presents small books on big topics and how they intersect with the world of business.

Individually, each title in the series provides coverage of a key academic topic, whilst collectively, the series forms a comprehensive collection across the business disciplines.

Careers and Talent Management
A Critical Perspective
Cristina Reis

Management Accounting for Beginners
Nicholas Apostolides

Truth in Marketing
A theory of claims evidence relations
Thomas Boysen Anker

A Short Guide to People Management
For HR and line managers
Antonios Panagiotakopoulous

Understanding the Born Global Firm
Neri Karra

Understanding the Born Global Firm

Neri Karra

Routledge
Taylor & Francis Group

LONDON AND NEW YORK

First published 2017
by Routledge
2 Park Square, Milton Park, Abingdon, Oxon OX14 4RN

and by Routledge
711 Third Avenue, New York, NY 10017

Routledge is an imprint of the Taylor & Francis Group, an informa business

British Library Cataloguing in Publication Data
A catalogue record for this book is available from the British Library

Library of Congress Cataloging in Publication Data
A catalog record for this book has been requested

ISBN: 978-1-138-21911-3 (hbk)
ISBN: 978-1-315-43617-3 (ebk)

Typeset in Times New Roman
by Taylor & Francis Books

For my brother, Fahri – for always being there for me

Contents

Contents

Illustrations

Illustrations

Preface

I first became interested in studying born global firms when I was a doctorate student at University of Cambridge. Initially, my thesis would focus on the foreign direct investment and internationalization processes of Turkish firms. Around the same time, I had founded our family business in leather products that was doing import and export from Turkey to Russia, or at least this is what I thought. As I delved into the literature, I would come to realize that the family business I thought was an import/export company was in fact a born global, as it fit the definition perfectly. This newly emerging stream of International Business piqued my interest, and I wanted to find out more, but while the topic being interesting, there was not much being written at the time about what the born global firm was, let alone about its challenges and what creates a successful one. This is how I changed the direction of my research from economics to entrepreneurship, from quantitative research to qualitative, and became a researcher in born global firms.

Since there were limited examples of companies that I could study at the time, I realized I had the perfect example in front of me: my very own family business. It would give me access to vast amount of data, allow me to interview and study key players, as well as see everything happening in real time. It was the perfect laboratory for a born global. For the next two years, I was proven correct, as the data I was receiving and observing was unique as well as important for contributing to our understanding of such firms. However, the challenge also remained that this was in fact a highly personal topic and a company, and whether I was able to remain objective when studying my own culture, my 'own people' and company. I would often hear these questions in conferences and workshops where I would present my findings, which eventually prompted me to write a paper on autoethnography: studying one's own culture, and explain how one can get the best out of the data and environment that they study, while detailing how to remain objective.

Lessons from the born global firm

This book offers a deeper understanding of what the born global firm is about, and what one can learn from one and how to even manage one. I analysed a company that became a born global firm, and at the time of my analysis, it was not clear to the founder himself that the firm was a born global one. This added another fascinating aspect to my study, because I got to observe how the entrepreneur managed this firm day to day, and later on expanded it globally. Therefore, this particular study offered me a highly unique perspective that not many researchers are able to get: a direct experience and witnessing of the born global firm. What I observed was that the idea of the business was deceptively simple: source fine leather and high quality accessories like zippers and clasps in Italy, manufacture wallets, mobile phone cases, and other leather fashion goods in Istanbul, and then sell them in Russia and the former Soviet republics. Four years later the firm would become highly successful, selling several million dollars worth of leather goods per year in a market that established global leather brands have found too risky. The most important characteristic was that no single bag or wallet was sold in the domestic market.

As this example shows, the rules of entrepreneurship have changed. This book helps us explore what gave rise to such firms, and outlines the factors that drive international entrepreneurship and tells us what the success determinants are for born globals.

Acknowledgements

The origin of this book goes back to my days as a doctoral student at University of Cambridge in the early years of the 2000s. My initial curiosity about entrepreneurship and the born global firm was sparked at a conference I attended as a doctoral student at Bocconi University in Milan, Italy, which made me change the direction of my thesis. My supervisor at the time, Dr. Christos Pitelis saw my genuine interest in this topic, and would allow me to change the direction of my research. I am grateful to him for first accepting me as a doctoral student, and for showing faith in my research. Professor Simon Bell would become my supervisor who guided me as I conducted my research. His insight, and friendly but firm attitude, allowed me to finish my thesis in under three years, while also being a Teaching Assistant in his Marketing classes.is where I would discover my passion for teaching. Professor Paul Tracey and Professor Nelson Phillips would become my co-authors as my research would turn into academic publications, and I am indebted to both of them for making research look fun and enjoyable. It is by working with them that I would learn how to publish, how to even present academic findings to an audience, and they would become highly influential in shaping me as an academic.

Finally, I would like to thank my external supervisor, Professor Tamer Cavusgil, who believed in my research from the very beginning, and would accept becoming the external supervisor. Over the years, and even more than a decade later, he remains a trusted mentor, an advisor, and someone whose advice I could count on at all times.

On a more personal note, I am indebted to my family: my parents and my brother especially, who have been very patient with me, as I embarked on an academic journey. Initially, they may not have understood why, as I could have remained and worked in the business side by side by them, but they would see that this is my passion, and would encourage me in pursuing my dreams and curiosity. I am grateful for their love and support, and knowing they will always be by my side. With such love and support anything is possible, and in the end all I can ever say is: thank you!

Introduction

The globalization of the world economy has had a dramatic impact on small- and medium-sized enterprises, both in terms of challenges and opportunities. The demise of the nation-state and the stand-alone firm as the primary macroeconomic players – combined with a decrease in protectionist policies and boundaries between domestic and international markets – has resulted in an environment where both small and large firms can engage in international activity from the outset. This is a relatively new phenomenon, one that was first mentioned in a scholarly article in 1988 by banker J.F. "Chip" Morrow, who pointed out that "booming international banking and financial markets produce unprecedented opportunities for today's entrepreneurs." In the years that followed, many other writers and academic researchers have become interested in the topic of international entrepreneurship.

The early body of work focused on the motivation, pattern, and pace of accelerated internationalization by small- and medium-sized new ventures, also variously referred to as born globals, global start-ups, instant exporters, micro-multinationals, and international ventures. In an attempt to understand such firms, researchers followed network theory, knowledge management and resource-based view, transaction cost theory, organizational learning, and product life cycle theory.

While insightful and enlightening, the research has lacked a unified framework to connect the antecedents, types, and outcomes of entrepreneurial activities pursued by such new ventures. In addition, most of these studies were based on samples of firms from the United States. The exceptions were studies of born globals in Finland, New Zealand, and Portugal. These studies and those that use US data have evolved independently of each other, leading to little congruence in theory building that would account for the potential differences in international entrepreneurship across countries.

These shortcomings suggest a need to pause and rethink the characteristics of accelerated internationalization in small- and medium-sized firms in order to develop approaches that combine different theoretical perspectives. This book attempts to do just that. In order to surmise what factors lead to international entrepreneurship and the success of such ventures that lack the experience and resources of established multinationals, I provide an in-depth case study of a single born global firm and the international network that surrounds it.

In Chapter 1, "International entrepreneurs: the founding and success of a born global fashion firm," I describe my in-depth case study of an international firm headquartered in Turkey with operations in nine countries in Central and Eastern Europe, Russia and its former Republics, the Middle East, and North America. I chose to study this firm because of its remarkable success since its inception, the diversity of its locations, my complete access to the organization, and my personal involvement and familiarity with the actors and main events of the case study.

In this chapter, I build on and extend the existing theoretical frameworks explaining the formation and success of born globals by highlighting the critical role of the domestic and foreign market environments. In addition to highlighting the importance of the founder's cultural competence in this form of born global firm, the study also reveals that the firm leverages complex networks whose members are tied together by common history and shared experiences.

In Chapter 2, "Building a business on ethnic ties: a study of the effects of ethnic networks on entrepreneurial activities," I delve deeper into the role of ethnicity and networks in born global firms. Despite the increased importance of network theory to explain accelerated internationalization, there has been very little attention paid to the role of ethnicity and social ties in the growth and development of international new ventures. Furthermore, while there have been a number of empirical studies of ethnic entrepreneurship, few have examined firms that have been highly successful or that have internationalized successfully.

I present the results of a case study where ethnic ties played a central role in its founding and rapid growth. The conclusion is that ethnic ties can be important resources in the founding of new ventures but that these same ethnic ties can become increasingly limiting as constituent firms grow and develop.

Finally, Chapter 3, "Cross-cultural research as autoethnography: the challenge and opportunity of studying your own culture in international management," introduces an interesting methodological issue I encountered while conducting the case studies. During my research, I was involved in a collaborative academic study with colleagues from

Canada and the United Kingdom. While working with them, I began to notice that I was part of a growing group of researchers who face a very different and much less understood problem than the more traditional one of being an outsider studying an unfamiliar culture: I was an "insider" researching my own cultural context and working to make the results meaningful and appropriate for international publication.

I researched firms that share my cultural and professional background and had to transfer my findings not only to my collaborators but also to the audience of international academic journals. Interestingly, while the problems of linguistic and cultural translation that face foreign researchers who carry out research in unfamiliar cultural contexts are increasingly well documented, there is not much said about those insiders, like me, who try to convey the results in an accessible fashion to the audiences of academic publications.

"Autoethnography" is a form of autobiographical personal narrative that explores the writer's life experience as a framework for understanding this challenge. It proposes that this relatively new methodology can be especially effective in the context of a carefully managed, multicultural research team. I draw on my experiences with an autoethnographic team to illustrate the opportunities and challenges of such an approach.

Combined, these three chapters contribute to the literature of accelerated internationalization in three ways: First, the thesis provides an in-depth case study of both a firm and a single network that have internationalized from inception. There are very few in-depth case studies that attempt to understand both international entrepreneurship and ethnic entrepreneurship. Particularly in a new area of research, such as accelerated internationalization, case studies provide an important foundation for developing a theory that can then be tested in wider, survey-based research.

Second, I have focused on a sophisticated, highly successful international network and a born global fashion firm that has grown very rapidly since its founding in April 2000. Case study researchers often recommend extreme or polar cases, because the entities of interest to the researcher tend to be more "transparent and observable," as Stanford University's Kathleen M. Eisenhardt wrote in 1989. In this case, the network dynamics that have driven growth, as well as the difficulties of managing them, are highlighted by the rapid expansion and success of the ethic network and the venture.

Third, the focus of my study is in a very different geographic location from that addressed in the existing literature. Whereas most of the studies to date have focused on ventures in developed economies in the West, I have focused on a company and a broad ethnic community that spans the developing economies in Russia, the former Eastern Bloc, and Turkey.

1 International entrepreneurs

The founding and success of a born global fashion firm

Iso Cara[1] was one of 360,000 Turkish Bulgarians who left Bulgaria in 1989 to make a new life in Turkey. He was a welder, who started an entrepreneurial venture with his wife. He opened a store in the luggage trade to benefit from the rush of Russian entrepreneurs with an idea that was deceptively simple: He would source fine leather and high-quality accessories like zippers and clasps in Italy, manufacture wallets, mobile phone cases, and other leather fashion goods in Istanbul, and then sell them in Russia and the former Soviet republics.

Years later, Cara's fashion firm, Neroli, is highly successful. He sells several million dollars' worth of leather goods every year in a market that established global leather brands have found too risky. And he does so without selling a single bag or wallet in his home market.

Cara's story shows how the nature of entrepreneurship is shifting. In the past, men like him would build their new ventures in their domestic market long before they'd expand globally. Now these same entrepreneurs have the opportunity and challenge of participating in a highly internationalized market from the moment they are founded.

These "born global" firms face a very different challenge from their more traditional, domestically focused counterparts, which leads us to ask: Why do they internationalize at founding, and what factors drive their success – or their failures? What are the complex dynamics surrounding this increasingly common form of business in our rapidly evolving business landscape?

International ventures from the start

> Geography, today, is history. But technology marches on, connecting us ever more easily and cheaply.
>
> – Newsweek Staff, 2004

The term "international entrepreneurship" first appeared in a short article by banker J. F. "Chip" Morrow in 1988. Since that early use, it has become an area of ever-increasing interest in the research community. Some authors have argued that the increasing globalization of markets has made international activity as much an area of activity for multi-national firms as it is for entrepreneurs. In fact, the idea that international trade is solely the purview of large multinationals has been challenged by the increasing involvement of young, small- and medium-sized entrepreneurial firms.

The early focus of research on the internationalization of large domestic firms led to an overemphasis on gaining "domestic experience" before moving into foreign markets. With the increasing globalization and saturation of markets, entrepreneurs often face competition both from local and international firms from the first moments of their existence. Gaining domestic experience, therefore, has increasingly less relevance for new firms, and the number of firms that begin their commercial activity in an international context can only be expected to increase. As a result of these trends, there is a critical need for further research that focuses on the internationalization process of new, small ventures.

Early studies on international entrepreneurship attempted to understand what leads to the emergence of this phenomenon, usually by trying to disprove the traditional frameworks of internationalization. While these early attempts have made important contributions, especially in terms of challenging the notion of traditional internationalization, interest has shifted to attempt to explain why born global firms become international new ventures from their inception and to determine the factors that drive superior international performance in international new ventures. Despite the work to date, there is still not a coherent framework that explains the dynamics of international entrepreneurship.

In addition to this, there has been some criticism of the ethnocentrism of the literature on international new ventures and the fact that the existing studies focus mostly on high-technology firms from a small number of countries, such as the United States. These limitations in the existing research suggest that there is an opportunity to build upon the existing work and to extend our understanding of what makes firms invest abroad early in their existence and what leads to their success in those foreign markets, by studying different types of firms in different geographic areas.

Cara's Neroli is one of those born global companies that derives its competitive advantage from the use of resources and the sales of its products in multiple countries. It produces and distributes high-quality leather goods, and, more recently, men's and women's clothing, with production facilities in Istanbul and sales throughout the countries of the former Soviet Union.

What determined the founder's decision to focus internationally from the beginning, and what were the key factors that led to the firm's rapid growth and profitability? It's those questions I set out to answer with my case study of this Turkish fashion firm. Unlike other research, which looks at established firms or, more recently, at the high-tech industry in the developed countries of the West, this study focuses on a new venture that spans a whole different geographical territory and provides an entirely different perspective.

Although the reasons for the increasing prevalence of born globals are complex and not completely understood, management researchers have made significant progress in understanding the most important factors. I will draw on my own work and on the broader academic literature to develop a framework to understand the drivers that lead to the increased prevalence of international entrepreneurship. I will consider the theoretical models and emerging research, methodology, data collection, and empirical context, and then analyze the results that lead to a model of the factors that motivate successful international entrepreneurs.

International entrepreneurship in context

The history of international business as a field has been largely one of attempting to understand multinational corporations. Why they exist, how they come to be, and what makes them more or less successful in their operations has formed the focus of decades of intense interest among researchers in management and economics. This focus on the international activities of large, mainly North American and European firms has resulted in the development of a body of theoretical work that goes a substantial way toward explaining the international activities of multinational corporations.

The Uppsala model remains the most widely recognized and cited model of firm internationalization, especially among entrepreneurship scholars. This model highlights how domestic and international operations relate to each other, and claims that business internationalization occurs in stages. That means a firm would learn and increase its foreign market knowledge over time, most likely first through domestic experience, and then would increase its foreign market commitment and expand slowly into distant markets.

This model remains an effective way to understand the traditional internationalization processes of firms. More recently, however, there has been an increasing recognition that firms are able to engage in international activities by skipping certain fundamental stages of internationalization, in particular foregoing the efforts of gaining domestic experience before moving into foreign markets. Technological change, combined with a decrease in protectionist policies and the boundaries between domestic and international markets, has resulted in an environment where it is not only large firms, but also small firms that consider international competition to be the norm.

This interest in the international activities of small firms has led to the development of an interest in the international activities of new entrepreneurial ventures – referred to as international entrepreneurship. This study focuses on new ventures that are variously called born globals, global start-ups, instant exporters, micro-multinationals, international ventures, and international new ventures.

While the above-mentioned terms all could be described as organizations that do business in multiple countries, there is no clearly accepted definition of an international new venture. It remains a matter of debate, with definitions varying from the very specific to the very broad, and with some going so far as to include corporate entrepreneurship. However, for the purposes of this study, an international new venture is defined as a firm that has at least 25 percent international sales within three years of founding and derives its competitive advantage from the use of resources and the sales of its products or services in multiple countries.

Theoretical models and emerging research questions

Forms of accelerated internationalization, such as international entrepreneurship, require alternative theoretical approaches from well-established explanations of multinationals and their international expansion. In 1994, Benjamin M. Oviatt and Patricia P. McDougall were the first to provide an explanation for international entrepreneurship. Their initial work identified rapidly changing computer, communication, and transportation technology, in addition to decreased protectionist policies, political economy, industry conditions, firm effects, and the management team as initial elements that lead to international entrepreneurship.

Despite the importance of this initial contribution, these elements are now accepted as accelerators of international entrepreneurship, rather than the dynamic processes that lead to the formation of international new ventures. In fact, in 2003, these researchers largely agreed with this later work in that they argued that such firms possess certain valuable assets, use alliances and network structures to control a relatively large percentage of vital assets, and have a unique resource that provides a sustainable advantage and is transferable to a foreign location – the same factors that were later identified as drivers of international entrepreneurship.

In addition to this, Shaker Zahra and Gerard George (2002) proposed a model of forces that influence the degree, speed, and geographic scope of corporate international entrepreneurship. They claimed that an organization's strategy and its political and economic environment moderate the effects of organizational factors – such as the nature of the management team and firm resources – on international entrepreneurial behaviour and competitive advantage. Their model, however, is directed more toward the activities of large multinationals and does not provide an extensive list of key factors that may influence new ventures to internationalize.

Among all the existing theoretical explanations of international new ventures, a limited number of themes have emerged. These include network theory, knowledge management, and organizational capabilities of firms. Network theory has been suggested as a much more suitable approach to explain international entrepreneurship and as a defining characteristic of such firms. McDougall, Shane and Oviatt (1994) claim that founders of international new ventures rely on networks in order to identify opportunities in the international business arena and that network effects have more influence than psychic distance on the choice of country for international new ventures. More recent authors have built on this early observation to argue that the uncertainty and risk associated with foreign markets can be overcome by using local market knowledge and the competencies of foreign intermediaries.

Knowledge and organizational capabilities have also been used to explain international new ventures. Existing research suggests that such firms are inherently entrepreneurial and innovative, leading to superior performance because of their specific knowledge about international markets and operations. Capabilities-based resources have been seen as especially important to international new ventures, as these help firms to facilitate their liabilities of foreignness and newness in unfamiliar markets.

These unique aspects and emerging themes in international entrepreneurship lead to the following research questions. The first issue that remains relatively unexplored is the question of what motivates entrepreneurs to seek out international opportunities rather than focusing on what would seem to be lower-risk domestic markets. Are there certain characteristics of entrepreneurs that lead them to seek international opportunities? Much has been written about the personality characteristics of successful domestic entrepreneurs, and there is a growing literature on ethnic entrepreneurship that provides some insight into the role of ethnicity in supporting domestic entrepreneurial activities. But there's little that tells us what leads entrepreneurs to brave the vagaries of international business. So given the already very risky nature of new venture creation, what characteristics make entrepreneurs willing to expose themselves to this additional risk or better able to manage the risk of these new ventures?

While the characteristics of the entrepreneur play a role and need to be understood in order to explain the phenomenon of international entrepreneurship, the environment also seems to play a role in encouraging or discouraging international new ventures. It is clear that improvements in communication and transportation technology, along with changes in international trade policy, have played an important role in encouraging international entrepreneurship. It is also clear that these new ventures are disproportionately represented in some sectors of the economy and in some countries. But what types of industries are most likely to encourage international new ventures? What government policies lead some sectors to be more attractive? Rephrased as my first research question: What individual and environmental characteristics encourage international entrepreneurship?

The above research question focuses on the reasons – both individual and contextual – that drive the decision to begin an international new venture. But this is only one part of the story. There is also the question of what drives success in these international new ventures. Are there critical competencies that an entrepreneur must possess in these very special firms? Are there identifiable resources and skills that underpin success?

There is a large amount of literature in international business that explores the kinds of competencies that lead to the success of large multinationals, but little is known about what is important for new ventures. A review of 27 studies that deal with born global firms provides the list of most critical success factors for such ventures. These are, in no specific order:

1 Managerial global vision from inception
2 A high degree of previous international experience on behalf of managers
3 Management commitment
4 A strong use of personal and business networks
5 Market knowledge and market commitment
6 Unique intangible assets based on knowledge management

7 High value creation through product differentiation, leading-edge technology products, technological innovativeness (usually associated with a greater use of Internet technology), and quality leadership
8 A niche-focused, proactive international strategy in geographically diverse lead markets around the world from the very beginning
9 Narrowly defined customer groups with strong customer orientation and close customer relationships
10 Flexibility to adapt to rapidly changing external conditions and circumstances.

Despite the significance of these success factors, there has been little empirical work done on the dynamics of this complex set of factors. As a result, there are several important outstanding questions: Are all of those elements important in the performance of international new ventures? Given that much of the research has focused on a narrow range of firms from a limited number of countries, are there other important success factors that have yet to emerge? And equally importantly, are some of these factors more important than others? These unanswered questions regarding the success factors in international new ventures lead to the second research question underpinning my study: What individual and organizational competencies lead to success in international new ventures?

Combined, these two research questions provide a framework for this case study. The research questions focus attention on aspects of international entrepreneurship that help to explain why entrepreneurs internationalize their new ventures and what the factors are that lead to success. The next section introduces the case study in an attempt to develop answers to these questions.

Methodology

I chose to carry a single case study of the international new venture, Neroli. In-depth case study analysis, as opposed to multiple case study analysis, provides a more detailed understanding of the characteristics of the context within which the theory was developed and, therefore, provides an opportunity to develop theoretical understandings that are simultaneously more situated and more tentative. That's because researchers are able to take into account the intricacies and qualifications of a particular context with a single case study. In addition, such studies provide access to more tacit aspects of the situation under investigations. This is the case here: Understanding international entrepreneurship requires rich, detailed, and comprehensive analysis that delivers the complex dynamics of the context within which it occurs.

The research site: an international fashion firm

I selected this case study for several reasons. First, the case had unique qualities that make it a logical candidate for what Kathleen Eisenhardt (1989) calls "theoretical sampling." Preliminary investigations revealed that the firm was a particularly good example of an international new venture or a born global. In fact, the firm had never had any substantial portion of its sales in its domestic market. It was, therefore, a completely international new venture. It was also a fashion firm based in Turkey with most of its sales in the countries that make up the former Soviet Union – a very different geographical location than much of the existing research on the topic. This combination maximized the potential contribution of the case study.

Second, as some of the research questions focused on the factors that determine success, it was very important that the firm I chose to study was highly successful. Neroli became successful in a short time and, therefore, provided an ideal context to investigate the determinants of success. In fact, Neroli's development trajectory has been remarkable. With limited resources and industry experience, the founder established the network in nine countries and went on to enjoy combined sales of almost 700,000 units of textiles and leather goods a year. This accomplishment is even more impressive taking into account that almost all the actors in this case study were new to the fashion industry when the firm was founded, and most had little business experience or personal wealth on which to draw.

A third important consideration at the time of the study was that the firm was only slightly more than a decade old. The founder was still the CEO of the company. This made it more likely that the details of the founding the firm, the early development of the company, and the motivations and direct experience of the founder were still fresh in the minds of the interviewees.

Finally, on a more personal level, I had been involved in the founding of the firm, having worked there as a translator for two years. Thus, I was familiar with the main events and leading actors. This also meant that I had good access to Neroli and the cooperation of its members, not to mention the cooperation of various international partners in Russia and Eastern Europe. I was also able to return to the firm on multiple occasions to gather more data and to reflect back understandings of the case.

Data collection

Semi-structured interviews were the primary source of data for this study. Initially, the interviews focused on the actors directly involved in the founding and ongoing management of the firm – primarily the owner and founder, his wife, the partners, main employees, and the first distributors of the brand abroad. Subsequent interviews were conducted with those who were less directly involved in the founding of the firm but still played a major role in the development of the Neroli brand (see Table 1.1 for chronology of events). The initial identification of interviewees was based on my personal knowledge of the firm. After the first round of interviews, I asked interviewees to suggest potential interviews with distributors and buyers of the Neroli brand. This sort of "snowball" technique is common in case study research.

A total of 42 semi-structured interviews were conducted in Russian, Bulgarian, Turkish, or English, according to the interviewee's preference. The interviews were taped and important segments of the interviews transcribed. Interviewees were asked to provide a detailed description of the evolution of Neroli and, in the case of buyers, a description of the history of their relationship with the firm.

In addition to interviewing, I also visited Neroli stores and major buyers in Russia, Kazakhstan, Bulgaria, Azerbaijan, Turkey, and Italy, which provided a good understanding of the context within which the born global firm developed and operated. I was also able to observe a number of meetings, including those called to draw up partnership agreements with independent buyers to launch Neroli in North America, the Middle East, and Azerbaijan.

I also had full access to all the documents, including agendas and business meeting summaries, private notes, and correspondence between key actors that depicted the milestones of the firm's initial founding in Istanbul and development of its international operations (see Table 1.2). Finally, in order to gain deeper understanding of the historical background of the born global firm, I consulted a variety of secondary sources on immigration and ethnicity, the history of the Balkan region and the Soviet Union, and the development of informal trade in Turkey in the 1990s.

Data analysis

The analysis of the data comprised four stages. First, I organized the case study data into an event history database. This was done by

Table 1.1 Critical events in the development of the network

	Approximate dates	Key events and issues	Countries entered
Stage 1: *Life in a new land*	1989–1992	• Cara explores the possibility of selling leather bags and purses to the Russian market. • Cara approaches a Turkish Yugoslavian immigrant who owns a leather factory in Turkey about a possible collaboration.	—
Stage 2: *The new entrepreneurs*	1992–1994	• The two men agree to open a small store in Istanbul (as a joint venture). The store sells a range of leather goods, and the products are targeted mainly at Russian tourists. • Cara works hard to build relationships with his Russian retailers and distributors. The business is very profitable, but Cara realizes he must reach more retailers and distributors if he is to reach his ambitions. This leads him to appoint a distributor in a number of Russian cities. He also develops relationships with distributors in Kazakhstan, Byelorussia, Ukraine, and Bulgaria.	Russia, Kazakhstan, Byelorussia, Ukraine, Bulgaria
Stage 3: *A new born global*	1994–1999	• The distribution network in Russia works very well. Cara decides to form his own brand (Neroli) and to source products from a much wider range of manufacturers. • The network expands to 77 stores across Eastern Europe, Russia and its former republics, incorporating around 750 people.	Uzbekistan and Azerbaijan
	Today	• The network attempts to expand distribution into the United States and United Kingdom but makes little impact. • Network members complain that they lack expertise in key areas such as marketing and finance.	Attempting to enter North America and Italy

Table 1.2 Data set description

Data source	Description	Number
Interviews	Company manager	7
	In-house company management (Istanbul, Turkey)	5
	Partners	3
	Employees	14
	Distributors (Moscow)	3
	Distributors (Azerbaijan)	1
	Potential distributors (Colorado, USA)	2
	Suppliers (Bologna and Florence, Italy)	7
Archived documents	Official contracts	12
	Meeting minutes	78
	Memos	23
	Faxes	255
	Emails	120
	Catalogues	45
	Financial data	2
Secondary sources	Literature on historical and political context at the time	–
	Newspaper articles	12
	Television programs	2
Website	Company Internet pages	7
	Other web pages	67
Other	Photographs of the distributors and the owner	32

chronologically ordering descriptions of events taken from the raw data – interview transcripts, interview and field notes, and secondary sources such as journalists' accounts of the political and economic conditions – and juxtaposing multiple accounts against each other to ascertain the degree of convergence. From this, I developed a narrative of the founding and development of the firm, including a general description of the broader economic and political context.

In the second stage, I coded the interview transcripts and notes for references to the primary concepts identified in the literature review and research questions. Coding proceeded, initially, on two levels. First, I coded using a lexicon of concrete terms grounded in the data I had collected (e.g. motivations, learning, risk, trust). Second, I used a lexicon of more abstract and theoretical terms found in the literature on international entrepreneurship, such as ethnicity, cultural knowledge, and network. That is, I drew on the existing frameworks for understanding the founding and success of international new ventures to see if they appeared in the emerging themes I was uncovering in the data, either as actual terms that were mentioned or as concepts or ideas that were referred to but not mentioned explicitly. I continued with the analysis iteratively, moving among data, emerging patterns, and existing theory and research until the patterns were refined into adequate conceptual categories.

In the third stage of data analysis, I tracked the motivations of the entrepreneur, the evolving business model of the firm, and the factors that emerged as critical to success, drawing upon the event history database from the first stage of analysis, interview transcripts, various interview notes, and secondary documents. In this stage, the intention was to uncover the evolving dynamics of founding and success in international new ventures – that is, to understand how the factors uncovered earlier interacted over time.

A fourth and final stage of "enfolding findings with the literature," to use Eisenhardt's (1989) words, brought together findings from the previous stages and related them to the research questions of the study. This permitted synthesis and the anchoring of findings theoretically. In addition, I examined private correspondence from the owner of Neroli and his partners, buyers, and distributors, as well as minutes of meetings and research notes, while actively observing meetings in which the new directions for the firm had taken place. The initial analysis revealed a number of reasons, both individual and environmental, that may lead to the emergence and subsequent success of international new ventures. These theoretical elements were then systematically coded, after which additional members were interviewed in order to confirm the results.

Neroli: a case of international entrepreneurship

Given the nature of this case, some understanding of the complex historical context of the study is necessary in order to show the multifaceted dynamics within which international entrepreneurship occurs.

There are two main events that set the stage for the development of the business model upon which the success of Neroli depends. First, between June and August 1989, more than 360,000 Bulgarians of Turkish descent who were living in Bulgaria were forced to immigrate to Turkey. The resulting exodus was described by John Pickles (2001) as the largest collective civilian migration since the Second World War:

> Lines of trucks, cars, and buses could be seen throughout the region, each piled high with people and whatever belongings they had been able to grab hold of and fit into the vehicles in a short time. Those who left abandoned home, land, and whatever they were unable to carry. In some cases, elderly and very young family members were also left behind.

This eviction/emigration put an end to an intense assimilation process that forced ethnic minorities, particularly Turkish Bulgarians living in Bulgaria, to change their names and prohibited their religious practices. Those who left Bulgaria settled either in immigrant camps set up by the Turkish government or moved into their relatives' homes, usually in informal, ethnic communities that had been established during other forced emigrations from Bulgaria, in 1954, 1968, and 1978.

The second important historical event that frames the study is the fall of the Berlin Wall in 1989 that set off the transition of Soviet Bloc countries from centrally planned economies to market economies with multiparty legislative democracies. The effects of this transition were dramatic, not the least in terms of the everyday lives of the general public, but also in terms of the rapid development of consumer options and entrepreneurial opportunities.

After the transition, numerous start-ups appeared throughout the former communist Bloc. While these were extremely varied, one of the most common forms of entrepreneurship was for citizens from the post-Soviet Bloc and Eastern Europe to travel to neighbouring countries. They would purchase goods and take them back for sale in their home countries in order to satisfy the rising expectations for Western-style goods that symbolized affluence, well-being, and financial status.

For Turkey, these new "luggage traders" were a welcome, if somewhat unexpected, export opportunity. At the time, Russian, Bulgarian, and

Romanian traders, in particular, went to Istanbul's Laleli and Beyazit districts to purchase clothes, leather goods, and bags, which they then took back to their home markets in their luggage. This trade, although largely unofficial, reached an estimated \$8.8 billion[2] by 1998, a significant figure in relation to Turkey's official total export figure, which ranged from \$20 billion to \$30 billion per year over the decade. These events provided opportunities for many Turkish businessmen, as well as for many post-socialist entrepreneurs.

Development of a born global firm

Cara, Neroli's founder, had three stages to go through on his way to being an international entrepreneur, beginning with life in a new land.

Stage 1: Life in a new land

Cara was frustrated with the limited opportunities available to immigrants in Turkey. Despite the fact that he had gotten a job as welder, his previous occupation in communist Bulgaria, his education and previous industrial experience were not recognized in Turkey. All that made it difficult for him to make a living, he said.

> The salary I received was barely enough, even though I worked as many shifts as possible. I realized that if I remained as an employee in any factory in any position, I would never be able to put my kids through good schools, provide them with good lifestyles. I had no other option but to go back to Bulgaria and sell the house, in order to create something, have my own business … do something on my own.

His frustration led him back to Bulgaria to sell his remaining assets in order to raise capital for a potential business. He then travelled throughout Eastern Europe and Russia, observing the market and contemplating his next step. He quickly identified Russia as having the most potential, because of what he considered its sophisticated and educated clientele, in addition to his familiarity with Russian culture and language. During his investigations of different options (including exporting pool tables and construction marble), he familiarized himself with the country and met important business contacts.

On one trip, he noticed a potential business opportunity that he would have missed if he had not actually visited Russia:

[I saw] many stylish women on the streets of Moscow carrying their belongings in plastic bags – not that they wanted to do that, but because they had no option. There were no purses or bags available at that time ... I saw an opportunity in the market, and I acted on it.

Upon his return to Istanbul, Cara got in touch with a Turkish Yugoslavian acquaintance he had met years before while on vacation in southern Bulgaria. He was an owner of a factory that manufactured leather fashion goods – with the brand name Jenni – for the local Turkish market. Cara was not familiar with the Turkish market and its regulations, and he did not have enough capital to start up his own business, so he offered his friend a partnership. It would consist of opening a small shop in the luggage trade area of Istanbul to take advantage of the increasing number of post-socialist consumers and entrepreneurs just starting to arrive. The owner agreed, on the condition that Cara would own only 10 percent of the Jenni store and would demand no percentage of the Jenni products sold.

Although this does not seem like a very exciting offer, in retrospect it was a real opportunity for an immigrant who had neither capital nor knowledge of the Turkish market. Cara asked his wife to join him in the Jenni store, as the majority of the luggage traders were women, and he anticipated that it would be much easier to gain and retain customers if they "worked hand in hand," as he said.

Stage 2: The new entrepreneurs

From the beginning, Cara created a special bond with his customers, no matter how few of the Jenni products they purchased. For instance, in his first store, there was a sign in Russian and Bulgarian saying, "Please come in for a cup of homeland coffee!" – a signal that he and his wife were from the same culture as their Russian customers. In fact, his wife confirms that there were many people who would drop by just for a cup of coffee at the beginning of the business. Cara and his wife also described how they would take major retailers for dinners and back to their home for drinks. They mentioned going on vacations with important retailers and going to their birthday parties and weddings.

From the beginning, the transactions between Cara and his Russian retailers were based on mutual trust. He often allowed his retailers to take the Jenni products on consignment, sell them in street markets in Russia, and then take the money back to Turkey. This flexibility, combined with the strong demand for leather goods in the post-communist consumer markets, translated into immediate success for the Jenni brand. Cara claims that not many of the shop owners trusted Russian retailers enough to provide goods in advance, mainly because it was risky and not accepted practice in Turkey. But also, those store owners did not understand Russian culture and found it difficult to determine who was trustworthy and who was not.

As the Jenni brand became more successful, Cara realized that in order to sustain the growth, he needed to move the products into shops, instead of selling through street vendors. However, he had a very scattered customer base, in an unstable Russian business environment. In order to offset these disadvantages, he decided to appoint one major distributor who was already one of his major retailers, in each main city where he was doing business. He wrote a detailed letter to all of his retailers explaining the change and why it would be better for them to buy from a distributor in Russia, instead of traveling to Istanbul. Not only was the response highly positive from his retailers, but it was also the step that established the brand in the minds of Russian customers. Here's how the brand manager in Moscow described it:

> Jenni was the very first branded leather goods to be sold in the country. It was Cara who put conditions on all of us to open up proper Jenni stores and sell the products in the stores, and not in the street market. I think this was the first step to build the brand, and people saw the stores, which immediately signalled that this is a brand name. It is a good quality brand name. Jenni was the first one in the Russian market – not only in leather goods – but also as a mere brand itself.

Stage 3: A new born global

Building on his success with Jenni, Cara decided to create his own brand and launch it internationally. Cara relied on the knowledge and capabilities of manufacturers in Turkey combined with raw materials sourced in Italy to create exceptionally high-quality leather goods that set his new brand apart in market. In addition, he relied on the knowledge and capabilities of the network of Russian distributors he had developed to distribute the Jenni brand when it was time to enter the market with his new brand, Neroli.

The reasons behind the decision to launch this new brand were complex. Part of the motivation lay in the desire to expand and grow, not shared by the owners of Jenni. Another was the desire to have something that was his own and that he could control as well as pass along to his children.

Although the two brand names operate in the same market using the same distribution network, their marketing strategies remain distinct. In fact, Cara's expansion into Neroli did not follow a particular geographic pattern but was based on his contacts and social ties. While he was introducing the first brand, Jenni, to the Russian market, he had formed a very large distribution network with reliable customers, who claimed that they would sell anything that Cara produced. Therefore, the area of operation has been geographically concentrated, with the new brand also selling mainly in Russia and its former Republics.

Cara attributes such specific regional expansion to his ability to speak Russian, his understanding of the culture, and his knowledge of the consumers in those cultures. However, he is also quick to note that such knowledge, in itself, is highly limiting, because it poses limits to expansion in other markets, such as those in North America and Europe. Despite the fact that there have been several attempts to expand, none has been successful, and Cara presumes this has to do with the fact that he does not speak English and can do only so much with a translator.

Today, the Neroli network (including outsourced production, in-house production, distribution, and retail) has grown to incorporate about 750 people and 77 stores in various countries in Eastern Europe, Russia, and its former Republics (see Table 1.3).

Learning from Neroli

This case analysis reveals four revolutionary changes driving the increase of international entrepreneurship. First, there was a shift from national to supranational powers in the macroeconomic environment, as has been suggested in the literature. However, it is obviously the case that not every firm or entrepreneur would translate available opportunities in the same way.

Table 1.3 Neroli's financial figures

Year	Total units sold (per year) Textiles – Leather		Total export value (USD)	% of change (annualized growth rate)
2001	–	49,816	$780,000	–
2002	51.557	182,262	$3.26 million	318.0
203	114,270	432,933	$8.70 million	166.8
2004	188,432	505,247	$11.935 million	37.2
2005 (as of Aug. 1)	275,973	125,100	$7.948 million	33.2

Moreover, the choice of destination also mattered. Why is it that certain entrepreneurs would choose a particular country, while others would not? Based on this, a second set of findings is presented that relates to the entrepreneur himself. In the case study, the entrepreneur was central to the development of the venture, interpreting the changes and opportunities in the external environment while possessing cultural competence, global vision, and the ability to recognize, access, and build networks.

Third, in addition to supporting organizational factors such as high-level and inimitable products and services, innovation, and smaller firm size, the case also revealed that entrepreneurial competencies and resources have a significant impact both on the decision and success of going global.

Finally, the analysis highlighted the importance of network forms of organization and related issues such as trust and risk, strategic group identity, and access to resources. The resulting model explains how and why networks are critical to the formation and success of this kind of an international new venture.

Determinants of founding in a born global fashion firm

The external environment consisting of both home and host markets are two elements similar to those already studied in the literature on international entrepreneurship. However, what this case reveals is a particular situation where the home country could be a foreign one for the entrepreneur, pushing him to markets that he is familiar with and, therefore, explaining the location advantage of foreign markets over domestic ones. Finally, the third force is the network form of organization that enables firms to expand into global markets despite their lack of resources.

The home country conditions

The local environment is an important element in the firm's strategic choices and plays an important role in explaining international entrepreneurship. Firms in small open economies with saturated markets and no protection policies are much more likely to internationalize from inception compared with other firms in large economies.

Similarly, in the case of Neroli, rising competition in the saturated and mature local market was one of the main push-factors for the entrepreneur to pursue global expansion. Turkish consumers at the time had limited purchasing power and perceived leather products as luxury products. If they bought them at all, it was during special occasions from well-known Turkish leather brands and leather bazaars, both of which have very high entry barriers. This restricted the entry of potential entrepreneurs and, therefore, led them to look for other opportunities. In other words, the Turkish local market was too small and saturated to support newcomers. As one entrepreneur explained:

> I could only make bags – part time, only – for some well-known Western brands. Although I have been in the leather manufacturing since I was 12, I could not make money in the Turkish market, because I did not have an established, well-known brand. It was not until the Russians came that I started to make money.

And similarly:

> Luggage trade was the best news in town for us. It created an opportunity for those who had limited capital, knowledge, and customers, to actually make some money – have a business. Russian customers meant more profit, bigger opportunities, and options.

Faced with a very small domestic market with no market protection from the national government, entrepreneurs turned to foreign markets, where they would not have had access previously.

In this case, however, there was an additional factor. The domestic environment was not a familiar one for Cara. Therefore, he formed partnerships with former immigrants from Eastern Europe, who were already familiar with Turkish business environment. He explained that he could not "even speak the language very well, let alone understand what all those legal terms mean." During my field trips, it was clear that he and the other managers still viewed the Turkish business environment as an unfamiliar and risky one, and, therefore, they had no interest in selling their products domestically. In fact, they said that the day they'd start selling products in the Turkish market would be the end of their business. They said that's because they still do not know how to deal with the dynamics of the Turkish institutional environment, despite the fact that it has been more than 15 years since their immigration from Bulgaria.

The host country effect

The impression may be that international entrepreneurs can easily and quickly learn about opportunities that lie abroad and, thus, find them easily and quickly. However, the truth is that most entrepreneurs are unlikely to go abroad. Those who do prefer countries with familiar cultures and where, as Zahra (2005) writes, "it is easy to understate the subtle and profound role of national cultures." The advantage of choosing culturally similar countries is that it reduces the liability of foreignness and allows the international entrepreneur to access and build foreign networks.

In the case of Neroli, the reason for the choice of market involves the entrepreneur's experience, culture, and interpretation of opportunities occurring at the time. What was interesting in this case is that the owner was much more familiar with the Russian and Eastern European culture than with Turkish culture. Not only did he have limited opportunities as a new immigrant in Turkey, but he also felt that the Turkish institutional environment was a highly unfamiliar one; hence, he decided to have a Turkish partner who knew the rules and regulations.

Cara expanded his business in an institutional environment that he was familiar with, one that he felt had low risk and high opportunity. Russia and its former Republics were now open and available for them to do business after the transition from communism to democracy. The locational advantage of the Russian market was its market size and potential high demand, in addition to the familiarity and knowledge many new immigrants had with the market and its culture. Either one of those on its own would not have the same impact or result.

Network forms of organizations

Although my primary case study was Neroli, the analysis revealed that the company was embedded in domestic and international networks of production and distribution that span traditional market boundaries. What allowed Neroli to operate internationally was not the fact that it had the necessary resources but rather that it was part of a network of firms that, as a group, had the necessary capabilities to internationalize.

In addition to providing support and encouragement that maintained motivation and overcome obstacles, the international and domestic networks of Neroli helped the firm globalize in three ways. First, they provided the necessary resources for the founder to exploit the available opportunities in Russia. It was the founder's social transactions involving trust and obligation that played a critical role in building the initial resource base. This enabled Neroli to acquire resources far below market price, in addition to knowledge about the institutional environment of Turkey and Russia. For instance, at the very beginning, Cara benefited financially from Yugoslavian partners, who owned Jenni and provided him with the knowledge of the Turkish institutional environment. Consequently, Jenni's owners capitalized on Cara's personal knowledge and cultural proficiency of the Russian market.

Second, the domestic and international networks created legitimacy and reputation for Neroli, as it was a small company without the necessary contacts and status in the market. When the founder decided to expand the operations to belts and bags, he was able to secure access to outsourcing associates through his Turkish partners, who were well known among the Turkish leather manufacturers.

Third, the network acted as a source of information about potential markets for goods and promising new business practices, enabling the network members to evaluate and act on the opportunities. An example of that was when Neroli expanded its business by selling men's clothing in the Russian market. The initial opportunity started with Cara's son, who went to a men's clothing manufacturer in Turkey and investigated the possibility of a Neroli men's clothing line. As a result, not only has Neroli expanded its product line very successfully, but its main distributor in Moscow also got involved in his own line of clothing.

Although these claims and examples may sound as if the international and domestic networks of Neroli will provide advantages on their own, this is actually not the case. The case analysis revealed that it was the entrepreneur who was the driving force behind the process of managing this network. Cara was the one who was involved in ongoing economic and social relationships in order to access, create, and manage his network. And he was the one who went to his Yugoslavian friends to propose the idea of opening a store in the luggage trade area, and then, after the entry to the Russian market, to assign one main distributor in each city. From the very beginning, the entrepreneur was active in terms of building and managing relationships. In fact, it has become very evident that the international expansion of the firm did not follow a particular geographic pattern but followed the entrepreneur's social contacts.

Overall, what fast-forwards the internationalization process of these firms is the fact that the entrepreneurs are embedded in domestic and international networks from the very early stages of their inception and that they have the necessary knowledge to use these networks.

Success factors in a born global fashion firm

Neroli's development and rapid success was one the reasons I chose it for my case study. The analysis revealed that the critical combination of cultural competence in foreign markets, combined with an ethnic and cultural enclave that supported entrepreneurship, explains much of the success of Neroli. The critical combination that leads to success in any international business is the degree to which trust develops and flexibility is instilled among network members connected through a shared history and common ethnic ties.

Cultural competence and language skills

One of the clearest findings was the importance of the entrepreneur's language skills and cultural competence, defined as a set of behaviours, attitudes, and policies that come together and enable a system, agency, or professionals to work effectively in cross-cultural situations, increasing the quality of services and producing better outcomes.

Cara's intimate knowledge of the language and culture of the former Soviet Union had several important ramifications. First, it provided the founder with the basis for developing a deep understanding of the market for fashion goods in this area. His cultural competence also allowed him to understand the direction of market evolution and to identify complementary products to sell through the rapidly developing distribution network. Established brands lacked that cultural competence and ability to tailor a market strategy to local conditions. They failed in the early years of the transition to a market economy, and Neroli succeeded. As a Russian distributor explained:

> When we first came to the luggage trade area, we were actually intimidated by the locals. They would not trust us at first, and neither did we trust them. ... It was much different with Turkish Bulgarians. They speak our language and come from the same background. It made things much easier.

This cultural competence could be seen in Cara's ability to manage complex social relationships with his network of suppliers and distributors – an impossibility for a manager without this intimate knowledge. The ability to create trust in potential partners also was critical to the strategy of Neroli. Although international new ventures are expected to possess superior resources, if they are going to offset the risk and uncertainty associated with doing business abroad, they need to rely on foreign distributors familiar with the institutional environment who, therefore, became intermediaries. The distribution network is one of the main success factors in the case of Neroli.

To generalize this point somewhat, one reason Neroli was such a success in a market that many internationally established firms found intractable can be explained by considering the relative risks facing these international firms versus those faced by Neroli. Cara faced a much lower degree of risk in these markets than his competitors. His ability to manage relations across a variety of stakeholders and to understand the market and political context meant that creating an international new venture was less risky for him than if he were to compete locally. This also meant that the learning curve that would normally be required for an international new entrant was not required. Neroli was born not just global but also culturally and politically competent. Therefore, the resulting argument is that cultural competence provides a measure of competitive advantage in international new ventures.

Collaborators

As previously mentioned, Neroli was founded on a strong international and domestic network of production and distribution. The underlying principle behind the success of the network was the fact that members shared a similar ethnic identity and were inclined to support one another. This ethnic identity served as a basis to begin collaboration and acted as "social glue" for the collaborations as they proceeded. The shared history and identity created certain linkages. I identified them as family-to-family linkages with members of the same immigrant family and ethnicity-to-ethnicity linkages with members who were not necessarily from the same exact geographical area but shared similar experiences, both as Balkan immigrants and "survivors" of communism.

For instance, although the Russian customers do not share the same ethnic identity as Balkan immigrants to Turkey, they tend to identify themselves as "one," because they were *bratyushki* (comrades) during communism. All had to survive the transition to capitalist regimes. In other words, their identities were based in shared experience as much as ethnicity. Similarly, the Bulgarian immigrants I interviewed tended to isolate themselves from the "local Turks" and claimed that they were more likely to trust either Balkan immigrants or Russians. Consider the following quotation from a Turkish Bulgarian immigrant who works with several Russian customers:

> We are very close and get along with Russian people. ... We have been through communism, but not only that ... during the communist times, Bulgaria was like the 16th Republic of Russia. ... We are born in Bulgaria, and this is where we had our personalities develop. No matter how much of Turkish ethnicity we are and no matter how long we live in this country, we will never change. ...

We understand where they [Russians] come from, what they want, what they cherish. We have the same integrity.

Therefore, the deep collaborations that characterize Neroli stem from the fact that these network members feel a common sense of identity based around their common experience of communism. The social networks and cultural practices of those people and regions that once were restricted from engaging in any kind of entrepreneurial activities now collaborate as actors in international trade and in new forms of ventures.

Conclusion

The Neroli case study and analysis is consistent with certain findings in the literature of international entrepreneurship literature, such as reliance on networks and existing ties, in addition to the home and host country conditions that act as accelerators of internationalization. However, the study also reveals new and exciting findings about international new ventures.

First, the existing claim in the literature that international new ventures go global is an over-generalized one, mainly because such an argument is based on a very concentrated sampling of firms from high technology industries in North America and Europe. This case study, however, reveals that there is a set of international new ventures that not only exhibit different dynamics from the ones already studied but also tend to internationalize based on their social networks and friendships, resulting in an expansion that is geographically concentrated around these ties. In the case of Neroli, such expansion was concentrated in Russia and its former Republics, because of the founder's social ties and network that provide the necessary resources for the company. As a result, I argue that while some firms may be born global, it is more accurate for many firms to say that they are "born-regional."

Second, the study also revealed that successful international new ventures are embedded in international and domestic networks, which will be explored further in Chapter 2. Although, studies have looked at the network approach in the explanation of the emergence of such firms, the literature does not argue that the firms are embedded in networks and that the entrepreneur and his social obligations are the driving force. However, this study reveals that the emergence of international new ventures relies on the network form of organizations. This is where the firm is embedded in both local and foreign networks and is more likely to be successful if the founder is able to access, build, and manage those networks.

Third, based on the previous two findings, there is an important type of international new venture with ethnic ties that provide the necessary resources to extend beyond its local markets. The importance of immigrant and ethnic communities and how they form successful ventures has already been detailed in the literature. However, this study reveals that these ethnic communities are significant enough to act in the international trade and play a part in the formation of international new ventures.

While the Neroli study has made several important contributions, it does have a number of limitations. First, as with all single case studies, it remains to be seen if the findings can be generalized. While they seem intuitively appealing and may have a place in the existing literature, some of the findings are the reverse of conventional wisdom. Obviously, larger sample studies will have to be carried out to test whether they can be generalized.

Second, the political context of the case is obviously quite unique. While this context highlights the dynamics of international entrepreneurship, it is equally possible to argue that this leads to very particular dynamics that, while worthy of study, are not representative of international entrepreneurship, in general. Third, the case study takes place over a relatively short time. Again, this is a strength, as this means that the events are fresh in the minds of the interviewees and that many documents and other archival data sources still survive. But it could also be argued that more time is required to make sure that this is not merely a burst of success soon to be followed by failure.

What is clear is that this is an increasingly important area of study. Entrepreneurship and international business are topics of great interest to practitioners, consultants, policy makers, investors, and management researchers. The intersection of the two provides a point of contact with real potential to contribute to entrepreneurship and international business – and to form a body of knowledge in its own right. For some entrepreneurs, forming global new ventures may be the best path to success. Both the existing literature and the findings of this study provide a framework of the dynamics of international entrepreneurship for further empirical testing to understand why and how someone might form an international new venture.

Notes

1 The names of the individuals and companies that were part of the studies reported in this book have been changed to protect their confidentiality.

2 These figures are based on the estimations in Turkey's Balance of Payments. In 1996, the Central Bank of Turkey's calculation for luggage trade exports was $8.8 billion, dropping to $5.8 billion in 1997, $3.7 million in 1998, and $2.2 billion in 1999. Suitcase trade earnings recovered slightly in 2000 to $2.9 billion.

2 Building a business on ethnic ties

A study of the effects of ethnic networks on entrepreneurial activities

For decades, researchers have observed that ethnicity, one's affiliation with a national or cultural tradition, plays a part in the acceleration of entrepreneurship. Some have gone so far as to theorize that certain ethnic groups, particularly among first- and second-generation immigrants, are more likely to create new ventures than others, even the population at large. These ventures are not just small businesses that cater to the needs of the same ethnic minorities; they are international enterprises founded on their ethnic ties.

But if ethnicity helps emerging entrepreneurs by helping them to advance their businesses through the networks they've created, does it lead these ventures down the road to growth and prosperity? Or at some point, do these ethnic networks limit and constrain them?

The research, with its narrow emphasis on how and why members of various ethnic groups *create* new businesses, doesn't say. It neglects other aspects of ethnic entrepreneurship. Thus, with my study, I began to redress this imbalance by going beyond an examination of the start-up phase and looking at the effects of the network dynamics of ethnic entrepreneurship from inception to relative maturity. I heeded the words of authors Linda Dyer and Christopher Ross (2000), and worked to develop "a better understanding of the social networks within which entrepreneurs continue to develop their operations."

More specifically, I explored the link between ethnic networks and entrepreneurship through an in-depth case study of entrepreneur Iso Cara and his international network of high-end fashion and leather goods producers, distributors, and retailers in Russia and Eastern Europe. The network is composed mainly of Balkan immigrants who left their respective countries and settled abroad. Their selective migration and settlement resulted in the emergence of trading networks, or trading diasporas, which "pursue different strategies than the majority," as Gopalkrishnan Iyer and Jon Shapiro wrote in 1999.

My study makes several contributions to the literature on ethnic entrepreneurship. First, I present a model of the role of ethnic networks in new venture formation and growth. The model builds on the existing literature but adds an important temporal dimension: the same ties that enable success during the formation and early growth phases come to limit and constrain the venture as it grows and develops.

Second, rather than study entrepreneurs as individuals, I studied a network and sought to develop an understanding of the network dynamics that characterize ethnic entrepreneurship. Third, I chose a sophisticated international network that has grown rapidly since its founding. Case study researchers often recommend extreme or polar cases, because the constructs of interest tend to be more "transparent and observable," as Eisenhardt (1989) wrote. In this case, the pace of the expansion and success of the network highlight the processes that have driven growth, as well as the difficulties of managing them. Finally, I focused on a network of ethnic entrepreneurs in a geographic location that is largely ignored in the existing scholarship. While most of the studies to date have been concerned with ethnic enclaves in developed economies in the West, I consider a broad ethnic community spanning transition and developing economies in Russia, the former Eastern Bloc, and Turkey.

I begin with a review of the ethnic entrepreneurship literature and present the research questions. Next, I discuss the methodology and introduce the empirical context of my study. Third, I present a model of the factors that influence the success or failure of such ventures and how these factors vary over time. Finally, I discuss the complex relationship between ethnicity and entrepreneurship, and suggest directions for further research.

Ethnicity and ethnic entrepreneurship

Ethnic entrepreneurship can be defined broadly as business ownership by immigrant and ethnic-group members. In an early work on the subject, Georg Simmel in 1950 focused on "traders" as "strangers" and the effect their status as outsiders had on their business dealings. More recently, Radha Chaganti and Patricia G. Greene (2002) defined the related term "minority entrepreneur" as any business owner "who is not of the majority population." Similarly, Greene and John S. Butler defined "immigrant entrepreneur" in 1997 as an "individual who as a recent arrival in the country starts a business as a means of survival." In all these cases, there is an attempt to differentiate between a majority population and some distinguishable minority population.

I follow researchers Howard Aldrich and Roger Waldinger (1990) in defining ethnic as an adjective that refers to differences between categories of people. When "ethnic" is linked to group, it implies that members have some awareness of group membership and a common origin and culture, or that others think of them as having these attributes. Waldinger (1986) built on this understanding to define ethnic entrepreneurship as entrepreneurship characterized by "a set of connections and regular patterns of interaction among people sharing common national background or migration experience." I start with this definition of ethnic entrepreneurship and add an element – the idea of mutual awareness. I thus define ethnic entrepreneurship as *entrepreneurship characterized by a set of connections and regular patterns of interaction among a group of people with a mutual awareness of group membership based on patterns of migration, common origin, or other cultural characteristic that separates them from the majority population.*

Ivan H. Light's *Ethnic Enterprise in America* in 1972 was the first major academic contribution to the debate about ethnic entrepreneurship. It led to the emergence of a stream of literature on the subject. The two most prominent early models are the "middleman minorities" by Edna Bonacich in 1973, and "ethnic enclaves" perspectives by Kenneth L. Wilson and W. Allen Martin (1982), and Kenneth L. Wilson and Alejandro Portes (1980).

The middleman minorities approach suggests that firms use ethnic entrepreneurs as negotiators to attract cheap labour in order to reduce their production costs. Unlike enclave theory, middleman minority theory is not concerned with where enterprises are located but with the role they play in facilitating markets. As the term suggests, studies concentrate on how ethnic groups act as middlemen in the movement of goods and services. Historically, members of these groups tended to be self-employed and to engage in activities such as labour contracting, lending, brokering, and rent collecting, primarily in the retail and service sectors. Entrepreneurs who occupy the middleman position generate entrepreneurial rents by negotiating arrangements between producers and consumers, owners and renters, elites and masses, and employers and employees.

The literature on ethnic enclaves, on the other hand, focuses on "immigrant groups who concentrate in a specific location and organize a variety of enterprises serving their own ethnic market and/or the general population," as Portes wrote in 1981. From this perspective, ethnic entrepreneurs accumulate social capital from their social networks in a given location and, therefore, are better placed than outsiders to take advantage of business opportunities in the enclave. In a similar vein, Light (1972) suggests that ethnic groups are likely to obtain a high degree of unity because of their marginalized status. These entrepreneurs and their co-ethnic employees also tend to benefit from the resources afforded by proximity and high levels of social cohesion.

While these contributions represent important steps in understanding ethnic entrepreneurship, they have also been criticized for their relatively narrow scope, and there have been calls for the development of more sophisticated and wide-ranging theoretical approaches. Aldrich and Waldinger's framework from 1990 can be seen as the first and most comprehensive attempt in this respect. These authors emphasize the often-disadvantaged position of ethnic groups in the countries to which they have immigrated and suggest that initial business opportunities are more likely to be found within ethnic markets. They also point out that further business growth is possible if ethnic businesses cater to non-ethnic communities as well, but they add that ethnic forays into non-ethnic markets are focused in those niches that a) are underserved or abandoned by large mass-marketing organizations, b) require low economies of scale, c) have low or unstable market demand, and d) are characterized by exotic demand.

Thus, a feature of this body of work is its emphasis on the challenges faced by ethnic minorities: racial hostility, prejudice, discrimination, and disadvantages in the labour market, such as a lack of language skills and recognized qualifications. Confronted with these circumstances, it is assumed that members of ethnic groups are often forced to turn to their family and community networks for employment and business opportunities. Nonetheless, and as Portes (1989) points out, there has been a gradual change toward a more positive characterization of ethnic enterprise as a mechanism for economic advancement, and research on ethnic groups has begun to move away from a focus on the hardships they face to the circumstances that may lead them to create alternative social and economic outcomes.

Most notably, Iyer and Shapiro proposed an evolutionary ethnic entrepreneurial business model in 1999 that was quite different from previous theories and arguments. Their framework considers ethnic groups not only as small businesses operating in niches and catering to the needs of ethnic clientele, but also as international enterprises. They argue that ethnic entrepreneurs tend to begin by supplying co-ethnic labour in an ethnic enclave. Their initial business ventures tend to focus on serving local markets within the enclave. Over time, these ethnic entrepreneurs might expand horizontally into non-ethnic markets and/ or by investing back in their homeland, and they may eventually expand the business internationally by leveraging their ties in their country of origin. The outcome is a set of lateral connections between multiple business interests in their country of origin and in their new country. The offshore Chinese population, for example, has been very successful at creating these kinds of business networks.

But while this emerging school of thought is an attempt to show that international ventures can be founded on ethnic ties, it assumes that such international expansion can be possible only because of the ties of ethnicity and friendship to the entrepreneur's country of origin. The existing scholarship does not yet include an examination of a set of firms that have successfully built international new ventures by relying on their ethnic ties to countries other than their country of origin. In addition, and as noted above, embedded in the ethnic entrepreneurship literature is the belief that ethnic groups are vulnerable, with limited opportunities and resources, and that the ambition to found a business venture stems from a lack of alternatives. Indeed, for the most part, it is assumed that ethnic entrepreneurial ventures "tend to occupy mainly traditional business lines dominated by small firms, and only seldom do they grow into larger firms and shift to more advanced and profitable business fields," as Miri Lerner and Susanna Khavul wrote in 2003.

I consider that the focus in the existing literature on small, local, specialized enterprises, and on why and how they are founded, is useful but somewhat limited. While many firms founded by ethnic entrepreneurs are small and focus on ethnic enclaves and specialized niches, even casual observation suggests that many are not. The question that arises, then, is what role do ethnic networks have in the founding and growth of the firms that do not fit this description? How well does the existing literature explain the dynamics of ethnic entrepreneurship that occur around these firms as they grow and develop? In this study, I begin to answer these questions by focusing on an international network that is not oriented toward an ethnic enclave and is not the sort of network discussed in the middleman minority literature. However, the central firm was founded by an ethnic entrepreneur and built upon his ethnic ties. Therefore, it is a very useful research site to explore the broader applicability of the existing models of ethnic entrepreneurship and to extend the discussion to these important alternative forms.

Methodology

It is worth noting that my choice of case study was based on both theoretical and practical considerations. From a theoretical point of view, case studies are particularly useful for theory building. Given the relative scarcity of empirical work in this area, case study research is arguably the most appropriate approach for extending the under-standing of ethnic entrepreneurship. From a practical point of view, there is very little reliable and publicly available data on the topic, particularly outside of North America and Western Europe, making broad demographic studies very difficult. And, in any case, the existing literature highlights the limitations of understanding ethnic entrepre-neurship in terms of size, prevalence, and key characteristics or traits.

Furthermore, while survey-based research was an option, my experience suggests that ethnic entrepreneurs are even less likely to disclose detailed information about their businesses than "traditional" entrepreneurs, with whom this problem has been widely encountered. Faced with these challenges in investigating ethnic entrepreneurs and their networks, researchers tend to use case studies to gain deeper insight. This is the method that I have chosen as well.

The research site: an international entrepreneurial network

In my fieldwork, I investigated all of the important ethnic ties that had developed around this one focal firm, Neroli. The network is shown diagrammatically in Figure 2.1.

I selected this case study for several reasons. First, my selection has unique qualities that made it a logical candidate for theoretical sampling. Preliminary research revealed that the network was a particularly good

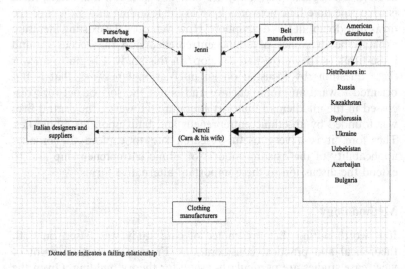

Figure 2.1 The Neroli network

case of an international ethnic network. The central firm, Neroli, had never had any substantial portion of its sales in its domestic market, and although it was founded in Turkey, it had always exported all of its production through the network. In addition, the size and the type of the network were very different from other studies, as it encompassed members from Turkey, Eastern Europe, and the former Soviet Union. The network was also very successful, having grown dramatically in a decade. These factors distinguish my case from more traditional research on ethnic entrepreneurship and increase the potential contribution of the case study.

Second, because the focal firm and network was only a decade old, most of the key actors had been members of the network since its inception and remained active within it. This ensured that the details of the early development of the network were still fresh in the minds of the interviewees and that the motivations and experiences of the members could be examined.

Finally, as I had worked for several years as a translator for the focal firm, I had attended many important meetings, was familiar with the development of the network, and knew many of the ethnic entrepreneurs who were network members. Because of this, I had extensive access to the key organizations, and the respondents provided me with virtually any information that I requested. I was also able to return to the main firm, Neroli, on multiple occasions to gather further data and to reflect back my understandings of the case.

Data collection

My primary data source consisted of semi-structured interviews with members of the network, related companies, clients, and suppliers. In total, I conducted 66 interviews with 26 respondents. Several of the respondents were interviewed on multiple occasions. A list of the interviewees is given in Table 2.1.

I began my study by interviewing the owners of Neroli and several of its key employees. During these initial interviews, I asked for the names of other entrepreneurs in the network, who were then contacted and interviewed. All of the entrepreneurs contacted consented to participate in the study. The advantage of using this technique was that it allowed relatively easy access to the main actors and made certain that I followed the most significant links of the network. It is very unlikely that respondents would have been willing to disclose information about their business ventures without the introductions from the founder of the focal firm. Using this technique, I found respondents to

Table 2.1 List of respondents

Respondents	Geographic location	Type	Number of times interviewed	Number of times observed at meetings
Iso Cara	Istanbul, Moscow and Italy	Face to face, telephone, email, fax	7	8
Wife	Istanbul	Face to face, telephone	3	—
Translators (Neroli)	Istanbul and Moscow	Telephone and face to face	2	5
Employees (Neroli)	Istanbul	Face to face	5	—
Employees (Neroli)	Moscow	Face to face	7	—
Kamal, owner of Jenni	Istanbul	Face to face	1	1
Belt manufacturer	Istanbul	Face to face	1	1
Bag manufacturer	Istanbul	Face to face	2	1
Leather supplier 1	Istanbul	Face to face	1	—
Leather supplier 2	Istanbul	Face to face	1	—
Distributor 1	Moscow	Face to face, telephone	3	1
Retailer 1	Moscow	Face to face	1	1
Retailer 2	Kiev, Ukraine	Telephone	2	—
Distributor 2	Baku, Azerbaijan	Face to face	1	1
Distributor 3	Kazakhstan	Face to face	1	—
Retailer 3	Chelyabinsk, Russia	Telephone	2	—

Table 2.1 (continued)

Respondents	Geographic location	Type	Number of times interviewed	Number of times observed at meetings
Entrepreneur 1 (luggage trade area)	Istanbul	Face to face	1	—
Entrepreneur 2	Istanbul and Moscow	Face to face	2	—
Marketing manager (Neroli)	Moscow	Face to face	3	1
Italian supplier 1	Firenze	Face to face	2	1
Italian supplier 2	Bologna	Telephone, email and face to face	4	1
Italian designer	Firenze and Bologna	Telephone, face to face, email	3	1
Italian supplier 3	Milano	Face to face	2	—
Men's clothing producer	Eskishehir, Turkey	Telephone	2	1
Store manager 1 (men's clothing line)	Moscow, Russia Sofia, Bulgaria	Face to face, telephone, email	5	—
Total			**66 interviews**	**24 meetings**

be very cooperative and was able to secure access to everyone identified as key players in the network.

I conducted interviews and collected archival data during several trips to Turkey, Russia, Kazakhstan, Azerbaijan, Bulgaria, and Italy. This phase of the data collection was greatly facilitated by attending and observing business meetings in which many members of the network were present from disparate geographic locations. In addition, I had a number of telephone interviews with network members in Chelyabinsk (Russia), Kiev (Ukraine), Bologna and Milan (Italy), and Sofia (Bulgaria). The interviews were carried out in the language of choice of the interviewee, whether it was Turkish, Russian, Bulgarian, or Italian. I also collected substantial secondary data in order to understand the economic and political context within which the firm was founded.

Data analysis

The analysis of the data comprised three main stages. In the first stage, I organized the case study data into an event history database. This was done by chronologically ordering descriptions of events taken from the raw data – interview transcripts, field notes, and secondary sources, such as journalists' accounts of the political and economic context – and juxtaposing multiple accounts against each other to ascertain the degree of convergence. From this, I developed a narrative of the formation and development of the ethnic network, focusing particularly on the role of ethnic ties.

In the second stage, I coded the interview transcripts and notes for references to the primary concepts identified in my research questions. Coding proceeded, initially, on two levels: using a lexicon of concrete terms grounded in the data (e.g. motivations), and using a lexicon of more abstract terms found in the literatures on ethnic entrepreneurship (e.g. shared history, common background, cultural knowledge). The analysis continued iteratively, moving among data, emerging patterns, and existing theory and research until the patterns were refined into adequate conceptual categories.

A third and final stage of "enfolding findings with the literature," as Eisenhardt (1989) wrote, brought together, iteratively, findings from the previous stages and related them to the literature on ethnic entrepreneurship. I worked back and forth between the raw data the narrative I had developed regarding the founding and development of the network, and the literature, in order to develop a model of the role and dynamics of ethnic ties in the development of the network. This allowed me to synthesize the findings and anchor them theoretically.

Neroli: an ethnic entrepreneurial network

Iso Cara was in an ideal position to build on his knowledge of the Turkish language and culture, and on his knowledge of Russia and the former Soviet Union, to forge an ethnic network that would support his new venture. As discussed earlier, he developed his network through opportunity identification and creating a special bond with his customers and retailers before creating his own brand and launching it internationally. When it came to his network, there were two other stages of development: leveraging the network and limits to growth.

Leveraging the network

The high level of understanding and cooperation between Cara and his partners underpinned what had become a very effective distribution network. Cara used this network to enter the market with his own brand, Neroli, which he created after disagreements with the owners of Jenni, who were reluctant to invest in the brand and expand into more countries. The disagreements between Cara and the owners of Jenni were obvious to network members, such as this Russian distributor:

> Kemal [the main owner of Jenni] is accidentally a businessman. He is in this business by a complete chance, and some other people are making money for him. He is not as driven as us and does not want to grow his brand or work any harder. He is a 9-to-5 person, who likes to have peace of mind. Unfortunately, this stubbornness or laziness has started to reflect very strongly into the brand. ... We are still receiving the same exact models of 15–20 years. ... No innovation whatsoever.

In addition to disagreements about investment and expansion, a further and perhaps more serious issue arose over Cara's wish to take part-ownership of the Jenni brand, which he believed was justified on the grounds that he had played such a prominent role in its development. The owners of Jenni refused, and this led Cara to create his own business, leveraging his existing contacts and the extensive distribution network that he had developed.

He subsequently named the new brand after his daughter, Neroli. Cara made two significant changes to Neroli that differentiated it from Jenni. In the first instance, the product range included a men's clothing line as well as a range of leather goods. Second, he decided to ensure that the products were of a higher quality, and to achieve this, he sought to use Italian suppliers and designers in addition to Turkish ones. The distribution network continued to take on new members, mainly in Russia, and in 2000 expanded into Bulgaria.

Although the two brand names operate in the same market and use the same distribution network, their marketing strategies are distinct. Cara is still involved with the Jenni brand and intends to continue promoting it. He said he feels obligated to the owners of Jenni, because they gave him an opportunity to establish himself when he first moved to Turkey, and he is still on friendly terms with them. However, several of the distributors interviewed said that without Cara's involvement, it is unlikely that they would continue to sell Jenni products in their stores.

Consider the following quotation from a Ukrainian distributor:

> This is not about a brand. It is much more about the people. All my transactions with the Jenni brand have always been with Cara, and I would not want to work with someone else. If Cara sells X brand, I will have that in my store. If one day, he sells clothes, I will sell that. I trust him. He is a good businessman ... a good person.

Ethnic ties and their limits to growth

The Neroli network, including outsourced production, in-house production, distribution and retail, has grown to incorporate about 750 people and 87 stores in Eastern Europe, Russia, and its former Republics. However, despite these successes, the reliance on ethnic ties has begun to inhibit the development of the network in some important respects.

First, most of the network members are from the same ethnic background, and Cara frequently recounted the problems of finding suitably qualified professionals, especially in accounting and marketing. He has also struggled to find a reliable English translator, which has proved a major stumbling block as he speaks Russian, Bulgarian, and Turkish – but not English. Indeed, he believes that not being able to speak English has become one of the most significant difficulties for his business:

> There are so many opportunities out there, but my hands are tied. I do not speak English. ... I cannot do this with a translator. It's not the same thing. The translator cannot be as energetic as me, and he or she cannot get across what I am trying to say exactly – every mimic, every eye movement, even the tone of the voice has a special meaning. ... My hands are tied without English.

Furthermore, Cara failed in his attempt to expand distribution into North America through a Moldavian/Russian immigrant based in Colorado, someone who had seen Neroli products at a trade fair in Moscow. It seems clear that this new member of the network does not have the capacity to build a strong presence in the United States. Similarly, Cara's recent attempts to source more expensive and sophisticated products, such as shoes from his Italian suppliers, have foundered because of a range of cultural and linguistic barriers. And while Cara is keen to expand into the United Kingdom, he has been unable to build the necessary alliances to enable this to happen.

Ethnic ties as enabling new venture formation and success

Neroli's development trajectory over the past five years has been remarkable. With limited resources and industry experience, Cara has established the network in nine countries, with a total export value of nearly $12 million during the last full year surveyed. This feat is even more impressive when one takes into account the backgrounds of network members. Like Cara, they were most often Balkan immigrants who were new to the fashion industry, with little business experience or personal wealth on which to draw. I was, therefore, very interested in the relations, transactions, and patterns of interaction within the network, which made this international expansion and growth possible.

The case analysis revealed three processes that both enabled the network to expand through new venture formation and assisted established members in a strategic sense. In the first instance, the data suggests most obviously that participation in the network allowed *access to resources,* which might otherwise be beyond the scope of members acting autonomously. A second enabling force concerned the high levels of *trust* exhibited among network members. Particularly striking was the speed in which trusting relationships developed, as well as the flexibility it instilled in network relations. Finally, *strategic group identity,* whereby the shared ethnic experiences and sense of community established a set of expected behaviours to which members were expected to conform, emerged as an important asset to network members.

Access to resources

The resource advantages of the network were most visible with respect to members at the margins of social and economic activity in their new countries. As noted above, immigrants are often excluded from mainstream labour and capital markets by their lack of knowledge and experience of the workings of their new context, and/or by weak linkages with "local" actors. But even where respondents occupied more privileged positions in their adopted homelands, there were clear resource benefits associated with the use of ethnic ties. The resources in question were sometimes financial, taking the form of debt to facilitate the formation or expansion of a venture, asset sharing, or preferential terms and conditions with respect to specialized inputs.

Perhaps more importantly, they also related to knowledge and information about market opportunities or the functioning of a particular market or industry. Longstanding network members who had faced similar or related issues in their entrepreneurial activities were able to pass on the benefits of their experience to others. This was particularly important for knowledge or processes that were complex and had significant tacit components, and were thus difficult transfer between individuals and/or organizations.

But as Cara's account of his early experiences of working with the Jenni brand illustrates, knowledge transfer was not based on altruism or the assumption that one should help others simply because they are part of the same ethnic group. There are costs associated with searching for partners and transferring assets, costs that are reduced by a reliance on ethnic ties. Moreover, the owners of Jenni hoped to capitalize upon Cara's cultural competencies and the possibility of expanding into the Russian market, thereby extending and strengthening their distribution beyond Turkey. In other words, the benefits of asset transfers accrue to asset holders as well as to the network members who acquire the assets.

Trust

The enabling role of ethnic networks extends well beyond resource acquisition and is central to the nature and form of the relationships between actors. This applies not only to the parameters or boundaries of the relationship, but crucially to the patterns of interaction and modes of behaviour among participants. In the context of this study, this manifested itself mainly with respect to the way that *trust* was developed and used. Trust is intertwined with conceptions of risk and can be thought of as the "willingness of a party to be vulnerable to the actions of another party, irrespective of the ability to monitor or control that other party," as Roger Mayer, James Davis and F. Schoorman wrote in 1995.

The offer of "homeland coffee" in Cara's store signalled that he and his wife were from the same culture as their Russian customers and could, therefore, be trusted to do business appropriately. The type of trust that manifested itself in Neroli was the type where, in the words of Roy J. Lewicki and Barbara Benedict Bunker (1995), "the parties effectively understood, agreed with, and endorsed each other's wants." In other words, members of the network were likely to forego opportunistic behaviour, not because of any penalties or rewards, but because it was understood to be the "right" thing to do. The trustee (the Russian distributors) recognized and accepted the validity of the trustor's (Cara's) needs, choices, and preferences, such that the trustor "can be confident that his or her interests will be fully defended and protected, without surveillance or monitoring."

On several occasions, Neroli's network members exhibited extraordinarily strong forms of trust. For instance, Cara and his wife would allow their customers to take the goods in advance and give them the money whenever they could. Such behaviour would usually be considered reckless, but in the case of Neroli, it was the only way they could initially do business. As Cara said:

> I am an immigrant and I know what it is to be robbed out of all the possibilities and opportunities you have. I knew that those luggage traders would not have the necessary money to purchase the goods sold in my store, because one wallet would cost about 30 dollars. This is way too expensive for them, because I noticed that the other stores were selling goods for 30–40 cents. ... At first, when I sold the goods on consignment, I told only my wife. If my Yugoslavian partners knew, they would have had a heart attack.

Similarly, from the point of view of Neroli's main distributor in Moscow:

> The luggage trade area at the time consisted of cheap but bad quality products. People who were coming from Russia to the area would not have much money, and that's the type of products they could only demand. Jenni products were 10 times more expensive among the leather goods being sold in the area. Not one of the Russian consumers would have been able to buy them if it was not for Cara, who trusted us and allowed us to buy the goods in advance. This is how I, like many other customers working with Cara, was able to start business, too. ... Before Cara, I worked with insignificant small shop owners who would never allow me to buy anything in advance.

On several occasions, members of the Neroli network exhibited extraordinary trusting behaviour, some of the key actors allowing themselves to be exposed to levels of risk that might be considered reckless in "standard" business transactions. In some cases, these risks were mitigated by the fact that the relevant parties were longstanding members of the network who interacted frequently with one another. For example, when it became apparent that distributing merchandise through street vendors was damaging the Jenni brand, Cara approached Ivan, the longstanding business partner, and asked him to set up a flagship store in the heart of Moscow. Ivan was required to shoulder significant financial risk but said he was willing to do so, because he "knew that he [Cara] would not let me down."

At other times, network members engaged in high-risk transactions, confident that their goodwill would be reciprocated in kind, even with little or no contractual protection in the event of malfeasance. This was exemplified most obviously by the strategy that Cara employed when seeking to expand into new markets. Rather than asking his partners to purchase stock in advance, he allowed the cost of the goods to be repaid *after* they had been sold. This immediately established Cara as a man of integrity and goodwill, and placed the relationship on a solid early footing. It also, of course, created a resource dependency, and a sense of obligation, which could be used strategically as the relationship developed.

A further benefit was that it allowed a much wider range of potential partners to be included within the network, because it was not a pre-requisite that vendors had access to substantial sums of capital. As noted, relevant industry experience was not necessarily a prerequisite – what mattered was that members felt confident that they could build meaningful and durable relationships with their partners, and that they shared an affinity and/or common bond of some kind. The ability to develop these relationships proved to be a crucial strategic advantage for the network as it sought to expand throughout Eastern Europe. Particularly significant was the bond that developed between Russians and Turkish Bulgarians within the network.

Strategic group identity

Related to the notion of trust, *strategic group identity* also emerged as an important enabling force. Margaret Peteraf and Mark Shanley (1997) defined this concept as a "set of mutual understandings" among members of a group, drawing the subtle but crucial distinction between mutual understandings and shared understandings. It is not a pre-requisite that members "perceive the group in exactly the same way [or] mirror each others' characteristics." What matters is that they "understand the behavior of other members and the underlying logic of decision making."

This proved vital to the effective functioning of the network, which formed the focus of this study, because it allowed members to confidently predict the behaviour of others without engaging in the repeated transactions normally required in the development of effective relationships. The process of identification also led to the development of shared norms and ways of interacting, which facilitated the transfer of knowledge and information within the network and imbued it with a robustness based around feelings of togetherness, mutual understanding, and common experience. This suggests a much more complex conception of ethnic identity than is espoused in much of the current entrepreneurship literature.

Social identification was crucial to the effective functioning of the network in another important respect, because it allowed members who did not conform to group expectations to be "punished" through a process of marginalization. The ability to sanction exhibitions of "improper" behaviour in this way provided a powerful incentive for members, especially when combined with the resource dependency described above, ensuring that actions remained within the boundaries of group norms and proving an important resource in the absence of contractual protection. This at least partly accounts for why malfeasance was largely absent within the network, as one of the Russian distributors explained:

> We invest almost everything we have for this business. It is our way to upgrade, become successful, and bring some bread to our family. ... We know that if we cheat, there is no coming back.... In fact, when we heard that one of ours had not been paying his money for a while, we all warned him, because his misbehaviour will affect our reputation as Russian partners as well.

Ethnic ties as constraining the network

When I began my study of successful international networks, I expected my analysis would focus on the positive and enabling effects of ethnic ties. However, I was surprised to see that the study also revealed the constraining effects of ethnic linkages, such as the one Cara developed. While Neroli has been very successful in Russia and large swathes of Eastern Europe, it has been unable to make inroads into the major international markets across Western Europe and beyond. As a result, the company has a distinct geography and is concentrated in countries with ethnic groups similar to Balkan immigrants, like Cara.

The hindrances were most apparent when members of the network interacted with prospective members who did not share the same ethnic identity. Such interactions tended to occur when Neroli sought to expand into new markets where it was not always possible to rely upon ethnic ties. Broadly speaking, three processes emerged that inhibited the capacity of the network to enhance its competitive position and acted as constraints on its development.

1 Membership lock-in

The first characteristic of network relations that constrains its development is membership lock-in. This takes place when individuals are retained by the network past the point in which it plays a constructive role in their development or after a more effective alternative has been found.

Once members are accepted into the exclusive circle of a network, there is a clear reluctance to expunge those who have outlived their usefulness or to switch partners when a more effective alternative emerges. Even when members step well beyond negotiated group norms and expectations and act in a way clearly detrimental to the network as a whole, expulsion is not always automatic. Of course, even ethnic networks have limits to their tolerance, and there are plenty of instances where members are excluded in response to a failure to honour commitments or because they are impeding network performance. However, this process appears more drawn out in ethnic networks than might be expected in non-ethnic networks, where the forces of social identification may be less strong.

The most obvious example of lock-in that I encountered in the Neroli network related to Cara's North American distributor, a US-based businessman named Anton he'd met at a leather goods fair in Russia at the beginning of 2004. Anton had immigrated to America from Bulgaria in 1991, and while he had no experience in the fashion industry, the two men built a strong relationship based in part on their shared identity. Cara was convinced he had found a trustworthy and reliable partner with which to realize his ambitions to export to the United States. After just a few weeks, however, Anton's lack of experience in distribution, in general, and the leather goods industry, in particular, became apparent. He did not have the competencies, credibility, or contacts to establish Neroli in North America. Indeed, Anton was able to sell only a fraction of the $50,000 of stock that had been advanced to him.

Even with all that, Cara was reluctant to break ties with Anton. It appeared that, for Cara, the nature of the relationship with partners was more important than the partners' abilities to improve the network's competitive position. For example, in the early stages of their business relationship, Cara drew comparisons between Anton's efforts to build a life for his family in the United States with his own experiences as an immigrant in Turkey. This sense of shared experience, dominating the relationship, may have been at the heart of Cara's unwillingness to sever the link:

> Anton is an immigrant like me. He knows what it is to struggle in a country that is not your own ... where you find it hard to fit in, where you have no other choice other than making money on your own. That's why he has no other choice but be truthful when he does business. This is how I know that he will stay true in our business dealings as well.

Of course, lock-in is a two-way phenomenon; not only does it protect modest performance, but it acts to obstruct members who seek to exit the network. The strength of these forces stems in part from the close and trusting nature of the relationships and from a more pragmatic set of motivations – the fact that members who leave the network can become competitors and form a significant future threat, given their intricate knowledge of the network processes and competencies.

This form of lock-in was evident on several occasions in the Neroli network. It was most notable in the long and protracted process that ultimately led Cara to loosen his links with Jenni, the leather goods company where he started, and to start his own rival brand. He had wanted to take this step for several years, but the role of ethnicity in the ties that bound him to the management of Jenni was very prominent, evidenced by his strong sense of loyalty and responsibility. Cara was sensitive to the position of his first business partner and agreed to develop a very different brand from Jenni, to focus on different markets, and to continue to promote Jenni in Russia.

As he said, "It is an obligation and a duty that I have to still help them in the Russian market. After all, they were the ones who helped me when I came here to Turkey and had no clue about how things worked."

2 Over-embeddedness

Harald Bathelt and Mike Taylor, in their book, *Clusters, Power and Place: Inequality and Local Growth in Time-Space* (2002), warn against the dangers of very high levels of trust and shared values in knowledge-intensive firms, which have the potential to lead to "blind confidence and gullibility" within networks. In these circumstances, over-embeddedness takes over, the rules and patterns of interaction that govern behaviour become rigid, and the flexibility to respond to changing conditions and contexts is inhibited.

With respect to the Neroli case, Cara's reaction to Avi, a US businessman who approached him in the summer of 2004 about distributing Neroli products across North America, neatly illustrates this phenomenon.

Cara realized that Avi offered tremendous potential for Neroli in North America, with his years of marketing experience and contacts with buyers of some of the largest and most high-profile US retailers, including Neiman Marcus and Saks Fifth Avenue. But a series of requests from Avi halted the relationship in its tracks at an early stage. First, Avi wanted written confirmation that the magnets Neroli used in its purses and bags would not damage cellphones or other mobile communications technology. Second, he wanted each of Neroli's products to include a warrantee so customers would receive a replacement or refund in the event of quality defects. Third, he asked for the weights and dimensions of every Neroli product, as potential buyers would request them. Finally, he asked for exclusive rights to distribute Neroli in the United States and that the current arrangement with his existing North American distributor be terminated.

From Avi's perspective, such assurances were straightforward and reasonable. He thought it was prudent to enact such risk management and obtain the kind of information necessary to trade in a litigious society and to negotiate a strong personal position. From Cara's perspective, that approach was not only alien but also contrary to the principles of mutual trust and reciprocity that underpinned his entire strategy for managing network relations. He interpreted Avi's requests as selfish, arrogant, and patronizing. Avi also asked Cara to sever ties with another network member he considered to be a personal friend. Despite its obvious commercial potential, Cara refused to proceed with the partnership with Avi.

The process that Cara relies upon to recruit new partners is based upon culturally oriented patterns of interaction. It has proved to be an effective mode of recruitment for partners with overlapping ethnic identities, in which both parties are working from a "script" of expected behaviours, and are sensitive to the idiosyncrasies of relationship building in that context. Avi, on the other hand, carried a very different set of assumptions about economic transactions and relationship building. In a litigious and consumer-oriented country, such as the United States, contractual forms of governance operate alongside businesses and often take precedence over trust-based ones. Thus, it could be argued that the entrenched nature of Cara's relationship-building routine led to a misinterpretation of Avi's behaviour and a failure to appreciate the context within which he was operating.[1]

3 Lack of competence diversity

The third constraining force is a lack of competence diversity. Cara's network showed a strong preference for individuals with a shared ethnic heritage. Thus, the network did not always have access to the key skills necessary for effective performance in the leather goods industry. And on several occasions, it was left exposed, mainly when looking to expand into new markets where the small number of Balkan immigrants made it difficult to leverage ethnic ties.

Neroli's reliance on the businessman Anton with respect to the US market is a clear example of this phenomenon, but there were many others. Indeed, the lack of competence diversity related not only to skills but also to specialized inputs. This stemmed in part from the difficulties that network members had in developing relationships with individuals and firms that did not share ethnic ties.

For example, one of the Russian distributors described the difficulties of sourcing goods from Italian suppliers, forcing Neroli to look for suppliers elsewhere:

> I don't have partners there [in Italy]. It just doesn't happen. It's hard. Italians are the best ones in shoe making, and the Turks can't even come close to them. They have a quality that other producers cannot even reach. ... But these dealings are not like the ones I have with the Balkan partners ... with them, it's different. We can talk about particular ideas, concerns, and frustrations ... they're very flexible [financially], whereas, you don't get the same flexibility with Italian businesses.

This difficulty of sourcing goods from Italian suppliers had significant implications for network competitiveness, as Italian companies tend to produce the best quality products in the leather goods industry. More-over, a reliance on ethnic ties led to a shortage of professional labour in accounting and finance, as well as marketing and technology. For example, the brand manager for Neroli was the daughter of a family friend of another network member. She had no marketing experience, but because her parents had worked in the leather goods industry for many years and were very successful, it was felt that she would learn the necessary skills quickly:

She is a very young and energetic person who has vision and is willing to work hard. She's never had any similar experience in branding or marketing, but I knew that she must have seen her mother and father managing stores as she was growing up and that she would be familiar with the business.

The dynamics of ethnic entrepreneurship

This case study supports the assertions of researchers that ethnic groups often struggle to "fit in" to their new countries, in part because of discrimination and in part because of the employment, language, and cultural barriers they encounter. Faced with such conditions, immigrants often look for alternative employment opportunities within mainstream labour markets, which often involves founding a business venture. However, a lack of financial capital and other resources, as well as knowledge of local markets and business conventions, leads many immigrants to rely upon ethnic ties in order to build their venture.

But the case also reveals that ethnic entrepreneurship may be far more ambitious and sophisticated than the existing literature suggests and that the depiction of ethnic entrepreneurial ventures as small enterprises exclusively serving similar ethnic needs and tastes is an outdated stereotype. The Neroli case undermines assertions like that of Lerner and Khavul (2003), that ethnic entrepreneurs "tend to occupy mainly traditional business lines dominated by small firms and only seldom … grow into larger firms and shift to more advanced and profitable business fields."

With respect to network relations, the analysis suggests that networks based on ethnic ties exert both enabling and constraining forces on members, which affect their capacity to combine resources in new ways in order to exploit market opportunities, i.e., their capacity to be entrepreneurial. As is noted below, these forces are not fixed, and they take different forms as the network and its constituent relationships evolve (see Figure 2.2). This is an important finding given the current focus on the enabling effects of networks as a strategic resource in the entrepreneurship literature and an almost complete neglect of their "darker side."

Upon reflecting on my data, it became clear that the enabling and constraining forces within the ethnic network had geographical and temporal components. I can say that, in general, the enabling forces were strongest in the initial stages of network formation and membership, where the network was concentrated in countries with high levels of Balkan immigrants and where access to new contacts and resources

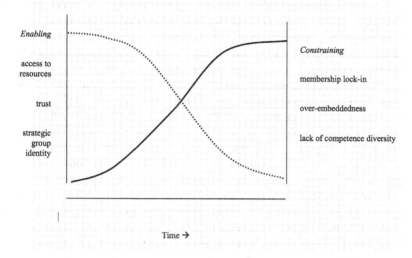

Figure 2.2 A schematic representation of the enabling and constraining effects of ethnic ties

played a crucial role in allowing members to build their businesses. Intra-network relationships tended to achieve a high degree of effectiveness relatively quickly, as members capitalized on high levels of trust and their shared strategic identity. But as the network matured, the benefits of membership were intertwined with a number of constraints, which hindered strategic flexibility. These constraints were not obvious in those locations where there were large numbers of Balkan immigrants, but they revealed themselves as the network looked to expand further afield.

As Neroli sought to move into Western Europe and North America, it was not always possible to maintain the ethnic "purity" of the network. And yet, there was a reluctance to enter into partnerships with people from other ethnic groups, even if they were placed strategically to help Neroli build competitive advantage. Moreover, where relationships with "outsiders" were established, they often faltered as existing members misinterpreted their behaviour and decisions. As a result, the network often lacked the competencies to compete effectively beyond the confines of its core markets.

While my study runs against the grain with respect to existing research in entrepreneurship, it is consistent with much of the organizational and sociological research on relationship building in general, and networks and social capital in particular. Amitai Etzioni (1996), for example, considers that at the core of strong communities of all kinds are boundaries that clearly separate members from non-members. Similarly, Janine Nahapiet and Sumantra Ghoshal (1998) argue that effective social relations are characterized by "closure" and a strong sense of identity, which necessarily creates boundaries between actors. Should these forces become too strong, however, network interactions run the risk of "producing forms of collective blindness that sometimes have disastrous consequences," as Nahapiet and Ghoshal (1998) wrote.

Thus, it seems that the key strategic issue faced by Neroli – how to bridge beyond its core ties in order to grow, while maintaining cohesion and shared purpose – is common to many networks and communities. In the case of ethnic networks, however, I suggest that this issue is particularly acute, because the forces of stasis, path dependence, and embeddedness tend to be stronger.

I recognize, of course, that I must be cautious about the findings and their implications; there are clearly limitations to a study that relies upon a single case over a relatively short period. First, as with all single-case studies, there are questions about whether the results can be generalized. While the findings seem intuitively appealing to me, and while they are in many ways consistent with the existing literature, some of the analysis contradicts conventional wisdom. Second, the geopolitical context of the case is unique. While I would argue that this context is helpful for exploring the nature of ethnic entrepreneurship, it is equally possible that, while worthy of study, the specific dynamic of the Neroli network is not representative of ethnic entrepreneurship, in general.

Finally, the case study takes place over a relatively short period. At one level, this may be construed as a strength, because the key events were fresh in the minds of the respondents, and many documents and other archival data sources were accessible to the researchers. But it could also be argued that a longer period is required to understand the complex social processes that were the subject of my investigation. In summary, while I am confident that my findings represent an important step in conceptualizing ethnic entrepreneurship, I do not claim to have produced a definitive account of the dynamics of ethnic networks.

Note

1 Of course, Avi must also take some responsibility for the breakdown of the relationship. But the onus was perhaps on Cara to appreciate the sensitivities of doing business in the United States, given his ambitions there.

3 Cross-cultural research as autoethnography

The challenge and opportunity of studying your own culture in international management

> Culture hides much more than it reveals, and strangely enough, what it hides, it hides most effectively from its own participants.
>
> – Edward T. Hall, *The Silent Language*, 1959

The phenomenon of autoethnography

The challenge of researching across cultures has received considerable attention in the international management literature. Discussions have focused on a range of issues encountered by researchers as they work to solve the difficulties with linguistic and cultural translation faced when researching in unfamiliar cultural contexts. The problem remains the central methodological issue in international management research and a significant challenge that requires careful attention to ensure success.

For a growing group of researchers, however, the problem is quite different. More and more, researchers in international management are "locals." For these people, the research is focused on their own cultures – familiar territory – with the results to be published in an international journal.

This phenomenon is driven by at least two trends. First, an increasing number of business schools outside of North America and Western Europe expect their faculty members to publish in international journals. These researchers naturally look to their own communities for sites to conduct research. Second, more and more researchers in North America and Europe come from diverse cultural backgrounds and find it convenient and attractive to return to their home countries to do research. For these people, conducting research "back home" allows them to collect data from novel settings and display their cultural and linguistic competencies. In either case, they face the problem of culture highlighted by cross-cultural researcher Edward T. Hall (1959): They need to learn to "see" their own cultures and then translate what they see for publication in international journals.[1]

This trend reverses the more traditional situation described by author Jean-Claude Usunier, who argued in 1998 that "international research is by its very nature comparative for the simple reason that the researcher has a different cultural background from the 'researched' field and informants." Research in this case is still international, but it is characterized by researchers who come from the same background as the research field but a different cultural background from the readers of the results. These researchers have the advantage of having "a name and a face in the local community," as Catherine Welch and Rebecca Marschan-Piekkari wrote in 2004. That familiarity brings about accessibility and a degree of insight not available to foreign researchers.

But this raises the question of what new challenges they might face. This is especially true for qualitative researchers. Malcolm Chapman, for example, describes his co-authors as "insiders," who, in studying contexts with which they are intimately familiar, have access, knowledge, and freedom of movement that allows them to develop particular insight into the contexts not visible to "outsiders." Being an insider is, in fact, suggested as a solution to many of the problems encountered by foreign researchers who try to conduct qualitative research in international contexts. But it also raises new issues around maintaining distance and managing roles as unbiased observers. This means that, for an increasing number of researchers, the problems faced and the sorts of solutions available are quite different from those discussed in much of the existing work on international management methodologies.

"Autoethnography" is a framework for understanding the challenge and potential of this approach to qualitative international management research. Autoethnography, a type of ethnography that uses the researcher's personal experiences as a source of data, is more than merely an insider's reporting of his or her own culture. This approach lies at the intersection of ethnography and autobiography, and involves integrating elements of one's own life experience while writing about others. It is important to be clear, however, that autoethnography is not to be used as a method in international management research. Instead, an increasing proportion of research in international management is taking on the characteristics of autoethnography, and it is useful to draw on that literature to understand the ramifications of this trend.

For international management researchers who conduct qualitative studies in their own cultural contexts, autoethnography provides a methodological framework for understanding and structuring their research. Even more importantly, it acts to sensitize the researcher (and potential readers of the results) to the importance of carefully managing the complex dynamics of this form of cross-cultural research. My approach follows the advice of Welch and Marschan-Piekkari (2004), who suggest that "while the use of methods from other disciplines is one way to broaden the practice of qualitative research in international management, such methods may need to be adapted to the particular context in which international business researchers operate." I will, therefore, introduce autoethnography as a qualitative research method and try to shape existing discussions of it to the realities of qualitative research in international management.

My observations grow out of extended reflection on my experiences while carrying out a research project in Turkey. During the research design and data analysis phases of the study, I worked closely with two collaborators, one Canadian and the other British. The project lasted nearly three years and involved in-depth interviews and participant observation followed by collaborative data analysis and theory development. The experience of managing this project and working cross-culturally and autoethnographically provides the basis for the identification of a number of central challenges and opportunities associated with this approach.

This study makes four important contributions to the literature on qualitative research methods in international management. First, it contributes to the growing literature on this subject. While qualitative methods are increasingly being used, their special characteristics have not received sufficient attention in the international management literature. Second, it highlights the increasing trend of researchers to explore their own cultural contexts with the intention of publishing their results internationally. Further discussion is required both to understand the ramifications of this trend and to provide sufficient guidance for researchers in this situation. Third, it introduces the concept of auto-ethnography as an approach to understanding this new trend in international management research. Finally, it outlines both the challenges and opportunities of this approach to research. While the more traditional challenges and opportunities of conducting research in a foreign context have been discussed at some length, little attention has been paid to more autoethnographic forms of research.

I will proceed in three steps. First, I will discuss autoethnography, focusing on its strengths and limitations. I will draw on the publications that exist on the topics of ethnography and autoethnography to provide a primer for researchers interested in the method. I will draw on my own experience of conducting research in an autoethnographic study in order to draw out some of the opportunities and challenges of conducting research in one's own cultural context in international management. Finally, I will conclude with some reflections on the broader ramifications of autoethnographic approaches in international management, based on the literature and my own experience.

Autoethnography and international management

Understanding autoethnography necessarily begins with a discussion of ethnography. Ethnography refers both to an approach and a final product. It is an approach in the sense that it is a method of investigating social reality and a product in the sense that the books and papers produced by ethnographers are referred to as ethnographies. David Silverman focuses on the latter in his book, *Interpreting Qualitative Data* (1993), when he describes ethnography as a conceptually derived description of a culture. James Clifford and Marcus George, focusing on the former in *Writing Culture: The Poetics and Politics of Ethnography* (1986), are more poetic:

> Ethnography's tradition is that of Herodotus and Montesquieu's Persian. It looks obliquely at all collective arrangements, distant or nearby. It makes the familiar strange, the exotic quotidian.... Ethnography is activity situated in the boundaries of civilizations, cultures, classes, races, and genders. Ethnography decodes and recodes, telling the grounds of collective order and diversity, inclusion and exclusion.

Ethnography is a research tradition that grows out of an interest in representing practices and understandings between cultural groups. It is based on systematic and rigorous observation and interviews, combined with the production of texts that work to translate the meanings and practices of a cultural group. As Silverman (1985) would say, in its concern with presenting cultural frameworks, ethnography is the most interpretive of all methodologies. Or, according to Clifford (1986), in its concern with presenting these frameworks to other cultural groups, it is the most literary.

The use of ethnography in management research is relatively rare – but not as rare as it its use in international management. Researcher Michael Rosen (1991) has argued at length for the value of applying ethnographic methods to the broader study of management in order to understand the complex social meanings and practices that surrounded certain workplace interactions. John Van Maanen (1979b), perhaps the most well-known ethnographer in management, argues that the aim of ethnography in the context of management research is to "uncover and explicate the ways in which people in particular work settings come to understand, account for, take action, and otherwise manage their day-to-day situation."

Ethnography also has its supporters in international management. As Malcolm Chapman and his co-authors (2004) argue:

> We need real, basic well-founded knowledge about what companies do and why they do it. Ethnographic research is one sure way of providing good detailed information.

That point is the same one made by Rosen and Van Maanen. Ethnography provides a way to explore the complex social climates of companies. It provides a way to highlight difference and to reveal the complex dynamics hidden by traditional methods. It is this sensitivity and exploratory nature that makes this sort of approach so valuable in international management research.

The move from ethnography to autoethnography occurs when the ethnographer's attention turns to his or her own culture. By this I do not mean simply self-reflection but theoretically structured introspection. As Deborah Reed-Danahay (1997) succinctly puts it, "whereas the ethnographer translates a foreign culture for members of his or her own culture, the autoethnographer translates 'home' culture for audiences of 'others.'" This double meaning of the study of one's own culture and the production of some form of more-or-less autobiographical text is summed up by Van Maanen (1995), who defines autoethnography as a specialized form of ethnography, where the culture of the writer's own group is "textualized."

But there is an additional use of the term that is important for us here. Mary Louise Pratt, writing in 1992, may have best exemplified this alternative definition:

> I use [autoethnography] to refer to instances in which colonized subjects undertake to represent themselves in ways that engage with the colonizer's own terms. If ethnographic texts are means by which Europeans represent to themselves their (usually subjugated) others, autoethnographic texts are those that others construct in response to or in dialogue with those metropolitan representations.

This definition focuses on the relationship between the two cultures and on the power dynamics and the intention to "engage" with the dominant culture. The texts are produced to appeal to the interests, concerns, and understandings of the dominant culture, not of the culture being studied. This aspect of autoethnography is critical to understanding the complex dynamics that occur when a foreign-educated researcher returns to study his or her local culture and successfully describes one of the important challenges that insiders face in such a study.

As I use it in the context of international management, auto-ethnography is a combination of these definitions: It is the generation of theoretically relevant and culturally sensitive descriptions of a researcher's own group for an international audience, based on a struc-tured analysis of that individual's experiences and those of others from the same cultural group. It is an attempt to share that experience with interested others. It does not mean that the researcher studies himself or herself, but that the researcher is an insider who can draw on personal experience, cultural competence, and linguistic resources to frame and shape research in a way that an outsider cannot.

From a methodological perspective, autoethnography reflects the fact that in some cases, the researcher and the subject can be one and the same person, leading to some constructive results. Particularly in a com-plex cross-cultural setting, this kind of approach provides an additional measure of ethnographic authority in that the researcher is accepted to be culturally competent and usually has the access to the research site. Therefore, it is expected that the problems of cultural competence, linguis-tic skill, and access would be reduced. The resulting research would have a greater degree of authenticity than if it was performed by an outsider, who would find it harder to develop a high degree of cultural sensitivity.

This approach does not come without problems. Several researchers have doubted the use of the self as a primary data source, for several reasons.

First, some writers argue that autoethnographers are simply being self-indulgent. The focus on one's own cultural group leads to an overemphasis and romanticizing of one's own cultural group, making autoethnography of little use in understanding the dynamics of another cultural group. One writer presents the process as a long and arduous journey, where it is all too easy to lose authority and "go native."

Other writers have suggested that autoethnography is difficult to evaluate, as the traditional criteria used to evaluate qualitative research are often not appropriate for autoethnography. An ethnographer's descriptions may be gaining cultural and linguistic competence in the field and in their adherence to time-tested methodological techniques, such as the field note and the "informant." But that doesn't make them valid. Thus, researchers are left without a clear way to legitimate autoethnographic work.

Finally, the depth of understanding of one participant's experience is a trade-off for an inability to move freely in the organization and observe others. The fact that the insider has a role makes it difficult to move through different subgroups of which the autoethnographer is not a member. In addition, role expectations are high, and behaviours outside of what is "normal" for the role may lead to confusion among subjects and the withdrawal of their cooperation.

Given this discussion of autoethnography, the parallels with qualitative work in international management, in which a researcher conducts a study in a local context for publication in an international journal, become clear. To a greater or lesser degree, depending on the research design, the researcher is acting as an autoethnographer who leverages deep cultural knowledge and linguistic ability while conducting a study. The researcher doesn't need to conduct an actual autoethnography but must draw on local knowledge and membership in a cultural group as one aspect of a study. The exact cultural and linguistic connection that provides the researcher with an advantage in carrying out the research also creates the sorts of difficulties described in existing discussions of autoethnography. In other words, this approach to international management research leads to the same kinds of opportunities and challenges as more traditional autoethnography.

But what exactly are the strengths and weaknesses of this sort of autoethnographic approach to international management research? What are the ways that researchers can use the advantages to their benefits, and how can they deal with the disadvantages of this method? In the following sections, I will discuss my own experiences in carrying out a qualitative case study in my native country and attempt to provide initial answers to these questions.

Autoethnographic research in international management research

I have been involved in several cross-cultural research projects in Italy and the United States, but what really shaped my understanding of this type of research was this case study of the international entrepreneur who founded the fashion firm, Neroli. The research project was part of a larger, multi-method program of research investigating ethnic and international entrepreneurship in Turkey among Turkish people of Bulgarian ethnicity.

Neroli is one in which I had worked as a translator and an interpreter; I also had family connections with the owner and managers. Thus, I was an autoethnographer in the sense that I was carrying out a study in my own cultural context – but also in the sense that I was studying a firm where I had worked and then returned to work as a translator for periods of participant observation.

My experience in conducting this research provides an excellent context within which to discuss the strengths and weaknesses of an autoethnographic approach. It is, in fact, what author Eisenhardt (1989) refers to as a "transparent" example, where the nature of the case highlights the dynamics of interest to the researcher. Based on my experience in conducting this study, I found both advantages and disadvantages in an autoethnographic approach.

Strengths of autoethnographic research

I have identified four strengths associated with autoethnographic forms of research that I believe are of particular importance in international management research: ease of access, reduced resource requirements, increased ability to establish trust and rapport, and reduced problems with translation.

1 Ease of access

Gaining access to a research site has been documented as the most crucial and problematic step in qualitative management research. In the case of traditional autoethnography, however, this problem disappears, as the research project generally grows out of a site to which a researcher already has access, rather than out of a theoretical interest that leads the researcher to search out a site. In fact, the researcher often begins with a site and then constructs a question that fits the research opportunity. Autoethnographic research, therefore, is, highly dependent on serendipity, e.g., does the researcher have access to a site that presents an interesting research opportunity? (This particular aspect also leads to certain limitations, which I will elaborate on later.)

So how does this apply to the type of international management research discussed here? In many cases, researchers from the local context will have connections that they can leverage in order to gain access to a firm. This may be a firm where they are already members. More likely, it is a firm with which they have some family or personal connections. This avoids the problems of dealing with official gatekeepers that plague foreign researchers entering the field through official channels. Official gatekeepers often allow foreign researchers so they can showcase organizations, or they allow them to talk only to certain organizational members. In the case of more autoethnographic research, the local connections of the researcher allow him or her to avoid these issues and allow access without intermediation by gatekeepers. This is hugely advantageous for the researcher.

In my case, because of my personal ties and connections with the organization, my access did not rely on official gatekeepers at all, so I could avoid the frustrating and time-consuming process of managing that relationship. Not only did I have access to an interesting organization, but the founder, members of the organization, and all of its alliance partners were happy to provide any needed information. I was also able to return to the firm on multiple occasions to gather data and to reflect back the understandings of the case. My pre-existing friendships with organizational members ensured that I always received an enthusiastic and interested reception.

In other words, more autoethnographic research in international management has the advantage of reducing the problems associated with gaining and managing access. This problem has been an enduring difficulty in international management research, and more autoethnographic sorts of research clearly reduce this problem. Having local contacts and personal relationships provides much better access both in terms of the organizations that can be accessed and in terms of the amount of access granted.

2 Reduced resource requirements

One of the problems faced by all researchers in this area is the expense and time demands of doing international research. Many interesting international management research contexts have markedly different social systems, literacy rates, cultural values, and status/prestige symbols from the familiar Western norms, and this complexity means that data collection is often one of the most difficult and important aspects of most international management research. It also means that it is one of the most expensive in terms of time and money.

Researchers, therefore, face the difficult task of securing sufficient funds to cover not only the basic costs of traditional research but also the costs of travel and accommodation in a foreign country and the very significant costs of translation. Based on my experience, more autoethnographic research helps dramatically to reduce the resource problems that plague international management research. In fact, being able to speak the local language and understand the local context has two mutually reinforcing effects. First, the cost of translation is avoided. This is a very significant and direct reduction in the cost of research. Second, being able to understand the language and context leads to a reduction in the amount of time needed in the field, which further reduces the resources required for the project. This two-pronged savings is part of the reason that anthropologists are routinely required to become competent speakers of the relevant language before entering the field.

This is particularly important given the rather fraught nature of obtaining external funding for international research. Qualitative researchers make note of the complex issues, such as loss of autonomy, time constraints that occur around framing the research proposal to obtain funding, politics, and pressure of accommodating the demands of national funding agencies. Anything that reduces the need for external funding, therefore, increases the likelihood of success in international research projects.

Even more importantly, many international researchers are reluctant to adopt qualitative approaches, as these projects are notoriously time-consuming and require extended time in the field. Given the ever-increasing focus on publication productivity, this aspect of qualitative research seems to be an insurmountable barrier to many researchers, with the unfortunate result that qualitative approaches remain under-represented in international research. More autoethnographic approaches reduce the amount of time required to conduct a study and make it more viable as a project for management researchers. This approach, therefore, provides an important impetus for the use of underrepresented methods in international management research.

To sum up, more autoethnographic approaches to international management research have several important advantages. First, the costs of doing research are reduced. This has the added benefit of reducing the unfortunate effects on research of the dynamics of securing funding. Second, more autoethnographic methods reduce the time in the field, making more qualitative methods more practical to adopt. Given the current imbalance between qualitative and quantitative methods in international management, this is an important additional benefit.

3 Establishing trust and rapport

International management research faces an increasing challenge as the focus of attention both for researchers and practitioners moves from a narrow focus on international business among developed economies to include more and more of an interest in transition and emerging economies. In these contexts, reliable statistical data is often difficult, if not impossible, to acquire, making a reliance on publicly available data impossible. At the same time, survey methods are simply not practical. In fact, the greater the difference between a researcher's home country and the foreign research site, the less likely the research methods and approaches used at home will be appropriate for the foreign field site. Informal interviews and participant observation are more and more often the only ways of obtaining accurate and reliable data. But this creates a very significant problem for foreign researchers. How do they manage to develop the level of trust and rapport needed to acquire the data they require?

This is a particularly important question because of the nature of doing research in emerging and transition contexts; respondents from organizations in these markets are often secretive and may even hide crucial information. They often are very unclear about what research is and have complex reasons for not wanting to disclose even basic information, such as the number of employees in a firm or total sales. The degree of trust and rapport that develops between the researcher and respondents is, therefore, crucial in determining the value of the research produced. And the likelihood of a foreign researcher being able to generate the level of trust and rapport required is often remote.

Autoethnographic research, where the researcher has the necessary pre-existing connections to the context and, ideally, to a firm and its managers, becomes one important solution to this problem. Researchers who have cultural competence and personal and family connections are much more likely to be able to create the level of trust and rapport necessary to gain access to the kind of data needed to build theory. Researchers without the necessary social capital are unlikely to get very far. A reflection of this is the increasing number of articles by Western researchers reporting the challenges of doing research in a foreign environment, adapting Western-style research methods, such as the interview or survey, to unfamiliar contexts, and dealing with complex issues of translation and contextualization.

The importance of establishing trust and rapport, and the increased likelihood of doing so if you are an "insider," has been discussed at some length in the literature. Hale C. Bolak (1996), for example, conducted an extended research project in her home country of Turkey and rapidly established high levels of trust among her interviewees. In fact, she became so trusted and built up such rapport that her respondents would happily share their most personal problems. The autoethnographic researcher, she wrote, was "able to ask relevant and meaningful questions to tap into their experiences, which made them feel understood and validated." It is hard to imagine a foreign researcher working through a translator and gaining this sort of position with respect to this group of participants.

Of course, my fieldwork had its downsides. At times interview subjects would be reluctant to provide me with certain information, despite our previous interactions and their familiarity with me. The sponsorship of the focal entrepreneur became critical at these moments, as it was his assurances that I could be "trusted" that led to disclosure. An additional problem occurred when I tried to explain the purpose of my research. The idea of a dissertation leading to a doctoral degree was unfamiliar to some of the respondents. Without the social capital built up over years of working with the company, there would have been no possibility of carrying out the research in these contexts.

4 The sticky question of translation

The issue of reliability, in terms of equivalence of language and instrumentation, has received particular attention among researchers in international management. More quantitative researchers have focused on conveying equivalence of language in their measuring instruments, which implies that the concepts and meanings used in the instrument must be equivalent across cultures. Researchers have tried to achieve such equivalence through a number of techniques, such as the use of high-frequency words and equivalent grammar, and by avoiding idiomatic expressions.

For more qualitative researchers, the problems of translating interviews and secondary sources of data have been a source of even more profound difficulty. Even carrying out an interview through a translator requires real skill on the part of the translator to convey nuances of meaning and context. Much of the most important aspects of the interview are lost as details and opportunities for probing questions are missed. For the interviewer, the problems of managing the interview through a translator are significant, not to mention time-consuming.

However, in the case of autoethnographic research, the issue of translation, equivalence of language and nuances, and applying surveys and interviews to "foreign" cultures are greatly reduced. Because of the fact that the autoethnographic researcher is studying his or her own culture, the researcher is able to relate to the subject matter and individuals studied, in addition to being able to conduct the data collection in the language of the interviewee. This results in higher reliability of the research and a more profound understanding of the research topic.

For instance, when I was conducting research in Turkey, Eastern Europe, and the former Soviet Bloc, I conducted all my interviews in the language of choice of the interviewee, whether it was Turkish, Bulgarian, Russian, English, or Italian. This immediately increased the efficiency of the interview process, put the interviewee more at ease, and prevented the difficulties of managing an interview through a translator. It also allowed the use of humour, which reduced feelings of awkwardness and any tension that might have existed at the beginning of the interview. Perhaps more importantly, having worked in those countries, I was familiar with the cultural nuances of individuals I was interviewing. This was particularly important when asking questions about sensitive topics like corruption. Without the necessary cultural and linguistic competence, an interviewer is likely to either abandon a line of questioning too early or to carry on and offend the interviewee.

Disadvantages of autoethnographic research

Throughout the process of carrying out my study, I faced three major disadvantages growing out of the autoethnographic aspect of my research: a lack of critical distance, ongoing role conflict, and the limits of serendipity.

Lack of critical distance

One of the most difficult problems facing ethnographic researchers, in general, and autoethnographic researchers, in particular, is the problem of creating and maintaining critical distance. In autoethnography, this problem often appears when the researchers find important aspects of the study to be obvious or natural, and, therefore, difficult to theorize about the research phenomena. They may overlook potentially important details or fail to report them, because of their quotidian nature. Alternatively, their close relationship with the topic of study may make certain features seem more salient and important than they really are. As a result, they may overemphasize these aspects in their work. Either of these difficulties can cause the resulting research to be less useful and less comprehensible than it would be otherwise.

In the case of my study, this problem occurred in both of these forms. On some occasions, I was unable to see what would be interesting about some aspect of the company I was studying. The mundane aspects that made a particular incident or comment important also made me unable to see its significance. On other occasions, I would find aspects of the history of the firm as being much more significant than they were, from the perspective of the project, because of my direct experiences with those events. Events in which I had played a pivotal role or that had been emotionally charged would take on an importance that reflected my personal perspective but did not reflect the potential contribution of that particular piece of data.

Role conflict

Autoethnographers, by definition, have a complex role in the situations they research. They are simultaneously members of the context in which they are immersed and outsiders working to conduct structured research activities. These two roles often conflict, with the research role interfering with the seamless achievement of membership, while the membership role prevents the researcher from carrying out activities needed for that role. Successfully conducting autoethnographic researching is, to a large degree, about managing this tension.

One significant problem that I encountered early in the research process grew out of the complex role I played. In this case, I had a long history with the organization and found it difficult to get certain members of the organization to take my researcher role seriously. Comments like, "but you know all that already," were common when I would try to get the participants to talk about their experience with the company's founding and early success. In addition, some research subjects were suspicious of how the data would be used, given my close relationship to the founder. The historical role of the researcher conflicted with the new research role in a way that troubled interviewees and made carrying out research difficult in the beginning.

The limits of serendipity

Previously I've discussed how autoethnographers study organizations with which they already have an existing relationship of some sort, such as an organization where they once worked, have some sort of family or other personal tie, or are currently involved. By studying an organization with which they are already connected, they are able to build on their social capital and take advantage of the positive aspects of autoethnography. But having this connection is, of course, largely a matter of luck. While these connections can be cultivated, they are fundamentally a matter of existing conditions over which the researcher has little control. In other words, it is a matter of serendipity.

This has two important disadvantages. First, there is no way for the researcher to make sure that the organization he or she has access to is in any way representative of the sort of dynamics the researcher is studying. Rather than the transparent example suggested by Eisenhardt (1989), the organization may be atypical in any number of ways. The convenience of the existing connection and the advantages of more autoethnographic forms of research can easily lead the researcher to exaggerate just how representative the organization is and lead to findings and theoretical generalizations that are simply not accurate representations of more general phenomena.

The second disadvantage is less complicated but could also be more problematic. Some researchers may not have any connections with interesting organizations. And, conversely, there may be very interesting organizations with which no researcher has any useful connection. Either situation leads back to more traditional research methods and approaches to gaining entry. Despite the disadvantages and limitations of more traditional approaches, there is no solution to a "social capital vacuum," and the use of official gatekeepers and translators is the best remaining option.

Conclusions

A summary of the advantages and disadvantages of autoethnographic forms of research is shown in Table 3.1. The advantages and disadvantages I have identified go some way toward answering the question of what, exactly, are the strengths and weaknesses of this sort of autoethnographic approach to international management research. When designing research projects or reading the results of this kind of research, it is critically important that researchers take advantage of the strengths of this method but also take care to manage the disadvantages, with a framework for explicitly managing the opportunities and challenges of autoethnographic research.

But this leaves the question of what researchers can do to minimize the disadvantages. International management writers commonly advocate collaboration among researchers from different countries, each one possessing the requisite knowledge of his or her culture. One writer prefers multicultural researchers, adept in the ways of many different cultures, to make up a team, but the practical problems of this are

Table 3.1 The advantages and disadvantages of autoethnographic approaches to research in international management

Advantages	Disadvantages
1) Ease of access	1) Lack of critical distance
2) Reduced resource requirements	2) Role conflict
3) Establishing trust and rapport	3) The limits of serendipity
4) Reducing translation problems	

often extreme. The first and most obvious point is to be aware of the problems. Thinking through the disadvantages and planning for them is an important first step. Second, it is possible to use a cross-cultural team as a partial solution. Using an "outsider" as a research collaborator helps the researcher to establish a critical distance, to reduce role conflict, and to balance the overly "local" opinion of the autoethnographer.

Obviously, this is just one step in the continued development of methods in international management. While I have pointed to the usefulness of autoethnography as a way of proceeding with research cross-culturally, there is still much to do. In particular, researchers need to continue to develop better approaches to managing cross-cultural teams and qualitative data analysis, and to focus more attention on the difficulties of communicating findings across cultures.

The challenges of conducting research and disseminating findings across cultures are tremendous. But the area is also of critical importance. Therefore, future research on this topic would benefit from much more discussion of what worked, what didn't, and what else can be done. The development of international management as a field depends on it.

Note

1 The degree to which this problem is evident in international management research depends, of course, on the research design followed by the researcher. In general, quantitative methods will suffer less, while ethnographic studies will be affected most intensely. Case study methodologies will be somewhere in the middle. At the same time, all forms of research that involve researchers studying their local context will suffer from these problems, to some extent.

Appendix

This study of the accelerated internationalization process in an international new venture has provided several contributions from both a theoretical and methodological point of view. From a theoretical point of view, it advances our understanding of international new ventures by investigating the entire start-up, growth, and management process. By looking at the process from an initial idea to the development and management of an international new venture, the study extends and develops existing findings that entrepreneurs in these ventures often rely on their ties of friendship and complex social networks in founding and growing a new venture.

But the study takes this idea much further. In addition to investigating network ties in general, the study investigates the founding and early success of an international network of luxury leather goods producers and distributors in order to show how the dynamics of ethnic ties facilitate management and growth in international new ventures. Such a study is unique in this area and helps us to understand the relationship between ethnic ties and building, developing, and managing international ventures. The addition of ethnic ties to the discussion of network effects in accelerated internationalization provides a much more powerful view of how at least some of these firms are able to internationalize, despite a lack of experience and resources.

Third, the study focuses on a unique industry and geographic region. Rather than studying new ventures from high-tech industries in Western Europe and North America, as is common in the literature, this study is of a fashion firm expanding across Eastern Europe, Russia, and its former Republics. The study, therefore, adds critical regional balance to studies on accelerated internationalization that is missing in the literature.

Fourth, by studying the development of a highly successful venture across a region, I am able to see that these ventures can come to be constrained by the same network ties that initially facilitated their founding and growth. In other words, while they are able to compete and expand successfully where they can build on their social network, they lack the capabilities to expand to other markets where their social networks do not extend.

From a methodological perspective, this study contributes in the following ways. First, it recognizes that there is a significant group of researchers who study their own cultural contexts and need to report their findings to an audience that is "foreign." I, therefore, introduce autoethnography, and particularly, autoethnography in the context of cross-cultural teams, as a potential method in international management research. There is little discussion of the problems of doing research "at home" or of the complexities of translating the intimate knowledge of a one's own culture to an international audience. This is, therefore, a first step in developing methodologies that recognize and even build upon this trend.

Second, it is an in-depth case study of both a firm and a network of luxury leather producers and distributors. The combination of levels of analysis provides a very useful vantage point to explore the complex social dynamics surrounding this venture. Also, as the research stream of international entrepreneurship is relatively new and there are few empirical studies available in this topic, case study research is recommended for further theory building. This in-depth case study is, therefore, an important addition to the literature.

In addition to the limitations of case study research, there is a need for future research in the area. This study proposes the term "born-regional," meaning that certain types of international new ventures are constrained by their capabilities. For instance, Neroli is highly successful in the Russian and Eastern European market and was able to achieve this success by relying on its ability to do business in that particular geographic area, but it has not been able to achieve success when it tried to go into the European and North American market. Therefore, my conclusion that these ventures are not "global," but rather "regional," needs to be expanded further.

Second, many of these new international ventures are family owned. They are often formed by entrepreneurs working through complex ethnic, family, and friendship networks. These networks both encourage international activity at the inception of new ventures and make it possible for entrepreneurs to do business internationally, despite their lack of resources. This leads to an important new focus for management research – the family-owned born global – that lies at the intersection of family business and international entrepreneurship. Interestingly, both of these research areas have traditionally received less than their fair share of attention, and both are areas of increasing interest for management researchers.

Overall, I believe that this study has made an important contribution in the area of international entrepreneurship, ethnic entrepreneurship, and qualitative methodology in international management. The study has contributed to our understanding of accelerated internationalization as well as highlighted a number of issues for further exploration. While much more work remains to be done, the study has served to highlight some important additional dynamics and to provide a more balanced geographic representation in the literature.

Bibliography

Adler, N. J., 1983a. "A typology of management studies involving culture," *Journal of International Business Studies*, 14: 29–47.

Adler, N. J., 1983b. "Cross-cultural management research: the ostrich and the trend," *Academy of Management Review*, 8/2: 226–232.

Agar, M. H., 1980. *The Professional Stranger*. New York: Harcourt Brace Jovanovich.

Aldrich, H. E., Waldinger, R., 1990. "Ethnicity and entrepreneurship," *Annual Review of Sociology*, 16: 111–135.

Aldrich, H., Zimmer, C., 1986. "Entrepreneurship through social networks," in D. L. Sexton & R. W. Smilor (eds.), *The Art and Science of Entrepreneurship*, Cambridge, MA: Ballinger, 3–23.

Ali, A. J., 1993. "Decision making style, individualism, and attitude toward risk of Arab executives," *International Studies of Management and Organization*, 23/3: 53–73.

Ali, A. J., 1995. "Cultural discontinuity and Arab management thought," *International Studies of Management and Organization*, 25/3: 7–30.

Almeida, J. G., Bloodgood, J. M., 1996. "Internationalization of new ventures: Implications of the value chain," *Frontiers of Entrepreneurship Research* [electronic edition].

Almor, T., 2000. "Born global: The case of small and medium sized, knowledge-intensive, Israeli firms," in Almor, Tamar, Hashai, and Niron (eds.), FDI, International Trade and the Economics of Peacemaking, A Tribute to Seev Hirsch, School of Business Administration, Academic Division, The College of Management, RishonLeZion, Israel, 119–139.

Autio, E., Sapienza, H. J., 2000. "Comparing process and born global perspectives in the international growth of technology-based new firms," *Frontiers of Entrepreneurship Research*, Center for Entrepreneurial Studies, Babson College, 413–424.

Autio, E., Sapienza, H. J., Almeida, J. G., 2000. "Effects of age at entry, knowledge intensity, and imitability on international growth," *Academy of Management Journal*, 43/5: 909–924.

Autio, E., Yli-Renko, H., Salonen, A., 1997. "International growth of young technology-based firms: A resource-based network model," *Journal of Enterprising Culture*, 5/1: 57–73.

Barrett, G. A., Jones, T. P., McEvoy, D., 1996. "Ethnic minority business: theoretical discourse in Britain and North America," *Urban Studies*, 33: 783–809.

Bartunek, J. M., Louis, M. R., 1996. *Insider/Outsider Team Research*, London: Sage.

Bathelt, H., Taylor, M., 2002. "Clusters, power and place: inequality and local growth in time-space," *Geografiska Annaler*, 84/B: 93–109.

Bell, J. 1995. "The internationalization of small computer software firms: A further challenge to stage theories," *European Journal of Marketing*, 29/8: 60–75.

Bell, J., McNaughton, R., Young, S., 2001. "Born-again global firms: an extension to the 'born global' phenomenon," *Journal of International Management*, 7/3: 173–189.

Bianchi, A., 1993. "Who's most likely to go it alone?" *Inc.*, 15/5: 58.

Birley, S., 1985. "The role of networks in the entrepreneurial process," *Journal of Business Venturing*, 1/1: 107–117.

Birley, S., Westhead, P., 1990. "Growth and performance contrasts between 'types' of small firms," *Strategic Management Journal*, 11/7: 535–557.

Bloodgood, J., Sapienza, H. J., Almeida, J. G., 1996. "The internationalization of new high-potential U.S. ventures: Antecedents and outcomes," *Entrepreneurship: Theory and Practice*, 20, 61–76.

Bodur, M., Cavusgil, S. Tamer, 1985. "Export market research orientation of Turkish firms," *European Journal of Marketing*, 19/2: 5–16.

Bolak, H. C., 1996. "Studying one's own in the Middle East: Negotiation, gender and self-other dynamics in the field," *Qualitative Sociology*, 19/1: 107–130.

Bonacich, E., 1973. "A theory of middleman minorities," *American Sociological Review*, 38: 583–594.

Bonacich, E., Modell, J., 1980. *The Economic Basis of Ethnic Solidarity: Small Business in the Japanese American Community*, University of California, Berkeley.

Bowersox, D., Cooper, M. B., 1992. *Strategic Marketing Channel Management*, McGraw-Hill: New York.

Boyacigiller, N. A., Adler, N., 1991. "The parochial dinosaur: Organizational science in a global context," *Academy of Management Review*, 16: 262–290.

Brown, J. S., Daguid, P., 2001. "Knowledge and organization: A social practice perspective," *Organization Science*, 12:198–213.

Brush, C. G., 1993. "Factors motivating small companies to internationalize: The effect of firm age," *Entrepreneurship Theory and Practice*, 17/3: 83–84.

Brush, C. G., 1995. "International entrepreneurship: The effect of firm age on motives for internationalization," in S. Bruchey (ed.), *Garland Studies in Entrepreneurship*. New York, NY: Garland Publishing, Inc.

Buckley, P. J., Casson, M., 1976. *The Future of the Multinational Enterprise*, London: Holmes and Meier.

Butler, J. S., Greene, P. G., 1997. "Ethnic entrepreneurship: the continuous rebirth of American enterprise," in D. L. Sexton, R. W. Smilor (eds.), *Entrepreneurship 2000*, Chicago: Upstart, 267–289.

Carsrud, A. L., Johnson, R. W., 1989. "Entrepreneurship: A social psychological perspective," *Entrepreneurship & Regional Development*, 1/1: 21–32.

Casson, M. C., 1982. *The Entrepreneur: An Economic Theory*, Oxford: Martin Robertson & Company Ltd.

Cavusgil, A. D., 1997. "Methodological issues in empirical cross-cultural research: A survey of the management literature and a framework," *Management International Review*, 37/1: 71–96.

Cavusgil, S., Tamer, Civi, Tutek, E., Dalgic, H., 2003. "Doing business in ... Turkey," *Thunderbird International Business Review*, 45/4: 467–480.

Cavusgil, T., 1980. "On the internationalization process of firms," *European Research*, 8/6: 273–281.

Chaganti, R., Greene, P. G., 2002. "Who are ethnic entrepreneurs? A study of entrepreneurs' ethnic involvement and business characteristics," *Journal of Small Business Management*, 40/2: 126–143.

Chapman, M., Gajewska De Mattos, J., Antoniou, 2004. "The ethnographic IB researcher: Misfit or trailblazer," in Marschan-Piekkari, R., Welch, R. (eds), *Handbook of Qualitative Research Methods for International Business*, Cheltenham: Edward Elgar.

Cheek, J., 2003. "An untold story?: Doing funded qualitative research," in N. K. Denzin, & Y. S. Lincoln (eds.), *Strategies of Qualitative Inquiry*, Thousand Oaks, CA: Sage, 80–112.

Chetty, S., Campbell-Hunt, C., 2004. "A strategic approach to internationalization: A traditional versus 'born global' approach," *Journal of International Marketing*, 12/1: 57–81.

Clifford, J., Marcus, George E., 1986. *Writing Culture: The Politics and Poetics of Ethnography*. Berkeley, CA: University of California Press.

Coffey, A., 1999. *The Ethnographic Self*, London: Sage.

Coleman, J. S., 1990. *Foundations of Social Theory*, Cambridge, MA: Belknap Press.

Coviello, N., Jones, M., 2004. "Methodological issues in international entrepreneurship research," *Journal of Business Venturing*, 19/4: 485–508.

Coviello, N. E., Munro, H. J., 1995. "Growing the entrepreneurial firm: Networking for international market development," *European Journal of Marketing*, 29: 49–61.

Coviello, N. E., Munro, H. J., 1997. "Network relationships and the internationalization process of small software firms," *International Business Review*, 6: 361–386.

Cross, T., Bazron, B., Dennis, K., Isaacs, M. (1989). *Towards a Culturally Competent System of Care, Vol. I*, Washington, D.C.: Georgetown University Child Development Center, CASSP Technical Assistance Center.

Dana, Leo P., 2001. "Introduction: Networks, internationalization and policy," *Small Business Economics*, 16/2, March.

Davis, K., 1997. "Exploring the intersection between cultural competency and managed behavioral health care policy: Implications for state and county mental health agencies," Alexandria, VA: National Technical Assistance Center for State Mental Health Planning.

Dawar, N., Frost, T., 1999. "Competing with giants: Survival strategies for local companies in emerging markets," *Harvard Business Review*, 77/2: 119–129.

Dijst, M., van Kempen, R., 1991. "Minority business and the hidden dimension: The influence of urban contexts on the development of ethnic enterprise," *Tijdschrift voor Economische en Sociale Geogra*, 82: 128–138.

Dimitratos, P., Johnson, J., Slow, J., Young, S., 2003. "Micromultinationals: New types of firms for the global competitive landscape," *European Management Journal*, 21/2.

Douglas, S. P., Craig, S., 1983. *International Marketing Research*, Englewood Cliffs, NJ: Prentice Hall Inc.

Denzin, N., 1989. *Interpretive Biography*, Newbury Park, CA: Sage Publications.

Denzin, N., 1990. "Writing the interpretive post modern ethnography," *Journal of Contemporary Ethnography*, 19/2: 231–236.

Denzin, N. K., Lincoln, Y. S., 1994. "Introduction: Entering the field of qualitative research," *Handbook of Qualitative Research*, N. K. Denzin & Y. S. Lincoln (eds.). Thousand Oaks, CA: Sage, 1–17.

Dunning, J. H., 1977. "Trade, location of economic activity and the MNE: A search for an eclectic approach," in B. Ohlin, P. Hesselborn, & M. Wijkman (eds.), *The International Allocation of Economic Activity*, New York: Holmes & Meier.

Dunning, J. H., 1981a. *International Production and Multinational Enterprise*, London: Allen and Unwin.

Dunning, J. H., 1981b. "Explaining the International Direct Investment Position of Countries: Towards a Dynamic Developmental Approach," *Weltwirtschaflitches Archiv*, 119: 30–64.

Dunning, J. H., 1993. *Multinational Enterprises and the Global Economy*, Wokingham: Addison Wesley.

Dyer, L. M., Ross, C. A., 2000. "Ethnic enterprises and their clientele," *Journal of Small Business Management*, 39/2: 48–66.

Dyer, W. G., Jr., Wilkins, A. L., 1991. "Better stories, not better constructs to generate better theory: A rejoinder to Eisenhardt," *Academy of Management Review*, 16: 613–619.

Earley, P.C., Singh, H., 1995. "International and intercultural management research: What's next?" *Academy of Management Journal*, 38/2: 327–340.

Easterby-Smith, M., Malina, D., 1999. "Cross-cultural collaborative research: Toward reflexivity," *Academy of Management Journal*, 42/1: 76–86.

Eisenhardt, K. M., 1989. "Building theories from case study research," *Academy of Management Review*, 14: 532–550.

Ellis, C., Bochner, A. P., 2000. "Autoethnography, personal narrative, reflexivity," in N. K. Denzin & Y. S. Lincoln (eds.), *Handbook of qualitative research*, Thousand Oaks, CA: Sage, 733–768.

Etemad, H., Wright, R., 2003. "Globalization and entrepreneurship," in H. Etemad & R. Wright (eds.), *Globalization and Entrepreneurship*, Cheltenham, UK: Edward Elgar, 3–14.

Etzioni, A., 1996. "The responsive community: A communitarian perspective," *American Sociological Review*, 61: 1–11.

Fiske, J., 1990. "Ethnosemiotics: Some personal and theoretical reflections," *Cultural Studies*, 4: 85–99.

Fontes, M., Coombs, R., 1997. "The coincidence of technology and market objectives in the internationalization of new technology-based firms," *International Small Business Journal*, 15/4: 14–35.

Garratt, D., Hodkinson, P., 1999. "Can there be criteria for selecting research criteria?: A hermeneutical analysis of an inescapable dilemma," *Qualitative Inquiry*, 4: 515–539.

Garud, R., Rappa, M.A., 1994. "A socio-cognitive model of technological evolution: The case of cochlear implants," *Organization Science*, 5/3: 344–362.

Geertz, C., 1973. *The Interpretation of Cultures*, New York: Basic Books.

George, G., Wiklund, J., Zahra, S., 2005. "Ownership and internationalization of small firms," *Journal of Management*, 31/2: 210–234.

George, R., Clegg, S., 1997. "An inside story: Tales from the field – Doing organizational research in a state of insecurity," *Organization Studies*, 18/6: 1015–1023.

Gilmore, A., Carson, D., 1999. "Entrepreneurial marketing by networking," *New England Journal of Entrepreneurship*, 2/2: 31–38.

GreeneP., 1997. "A resource-based approach to ethnic business sponsorship: A consideration of Ismaili-Pakistani immigrants," *Journal of Small Business Management*, 35: 58–71.

Greve, A., Salaff, J. W., 2003. "Social networks and entrepreneurship," *Entrepreneurship, Theory and Practice*, 28/1: 1–22.

Guba, E.G., Lincoln, Y. S., 1989. *Fourth Generation Evaluation*. Newbury Park, CA: Sage.

Gummeson, E., 1991. *Qualitative Methods in Management Research*, London: Sage.

Hall, E. T., 1959. *The Silent Language*, New York: Doubleday.

Hansen, M.T., 1999. "The search-transfer problem: The role of weak ties in sharing knowledge across organization subunits," *Administrative Science Quarterly*, 44: 82–111.

Hardy, C., Phillips, N., Lawrence, T., 1998. "Distinguishing trust and power in interorganizational relations: Forms and facades of trust," in C. Lane & R. Bachmann (eds.), *Trust Within and Between Organizations: Conceptual Issues and Empirical Applications*, 64–87.

Hashai, N., Almor, T., 2004. "Gradually internationalizing born global firms – An oxymoron?" *International Business Review*, 13/4: 465–483.

Hayano, D. M., 1982. "Auto-ethnography," *Human Organization*, 38: 99–104.

Hayashi, S., 1988. *Culture and Management in Japan*, Tokyo: University of Tokyo Press.

Hirsch, R., Honig-Haftel, S., McDougall, P., Oviatt, B., 1996. "International entrepreneurship: Past, present and future," *Entrepreneurship Theory and Practice*, 20/4: 5.

Hofstede, G. H., 1979. "Value systems in forty countries: Interpretation, validation and consequences for theory," in L. H. Eckensberger, W. J. Lonner, & Y. H. Poortinga (eds.), *Cross-Cultural Contributions to Psychology*. Lisse, Netherlands: Sweets and Zeitlinger, 389–407.

Hofstede, G. H., 1983. "The cultural relativity of organizational practices and theories," *Journal of International Business Studies*, 14/2: 75–89.

Hofstede, G. H., 1984. *Culture's Consequences: International Differences in Work-Related Values*. Beverly Hills, CA: Sage.

Holmlund, M., Kock, S., 1998. "Relationships and the internationalisation of Finnish small and medium-sized companies," *International Small Business Journal*, 16, 46–63.

Hymer, S. S., 1976. *The International Operation of National Firms: A Study of Direct Foreign Investment* (PhD Thesis 1960), published Cambridge, MA.

Isaacs, M., Benjamin, M., 1991. "Towards a culturally competent system of care, volume II, programs which utilize culturally competent principles," Washington, D.C.: Georgetown University Child Development Center, CASSP Technical Assistance Center.

Iyer, G., Shapiro, J., 1999. "Ethnic entrepreneurial and marketing systems: Implications for the global economy," *Journal of International Marketing*, 7/3: 83–110.

Jackall, R., 1989. *Moral Mazes: The World of Corporate Managers*. Oxford University Press.

Johanson, J., Vahlne, J., 1977. "The internationalization process of the firm, a model of knowledge development and increasing foreign market commitment," *Journal of International Business Studies*, spring/summer.

Johanson, J., Vahlne, J. E., 1990. "The mechanism of internationalization," *International Marketing Review*, 7/4: 11–24.

Johanson, J., Vahlne, J. E., 2003. "Business relationship learning and commitment in the internationalization process," *Journal of International Entrepreneurship*, 1: 83–101.

Johanson, J., Wiedersheim-Paul, F., 1993. "The internationalization of the firm: Four Swedish cases," P. J. Buckley & P. N. Ghauri (eds.), 16–31. (Reprinted from *Journal of Management Studies*, 1975, 12, October: 305–322.)

Jolly, V. K., Alahunta, M., Jeannet, J. P., 1992. "Challenging the incumbents: How high technology start-ups compete globally," *Journal of Strategic Change*, 1: 71–82.

Kaplan, D.H., 1998. "The spatial structure of urban ethnic economies," *Urban Geography*, 19: 489–501.

Karra, N., Phillips, N., 2004. "Entrepreneurship goes global," *Ivey Business Journal*, 68/8.

Knight, G., 2000. "Entrepreneurship and marketing strategy: The SME under globalization," *Journal of International Marketing*, 8/2: 12–32.

Knight, G. G., Cavusgil, S. T., 1996. "The born global firm: A challenge to traditional internationalization theory," *Advances in International Marketing*, 8: 11–26.

Knight, G., Cavusgil, T., 2004. "Innovation, organizational capabilities and the born global firm," *Journal of International Business Studies*, 35/4: 1–18.

Knight, J., Bell, J., McNaughton, R., 2001. "The born global phenomenon: Re-birth of an old concept?" in M. Jones & P. Dimitratos (eds.), *Researching New Frontiers*, 4th McGill Conference on International Entrepreneurship, 2: 113–125.

Kuemmerle, W., 2002. "Home base and knowledge management in international ventures," *Journal of Business Venturing*, 17: 99–122.

Larimo, J., 2001. "Internationalization of SMEs – Two case studies of Finnish born global firms," paper presented at the CIMaR Annual Conference in Sydney, Australia.

Larson, A., 1992. "Network dyads in entrepreneurial settings: A study of the governance of exchange relationships," *Administrative Science Quarterly*, 37: 76–104.

Lerner, M., Khavul, S., 2003. "Beating the odds in immigrant entrepreneurship: How does founder human capital compare to institutional social capital in improving the survival of immigrant owned businesses?" Paper presented at the Babson Entrepreneurship Conference, Babson College, June 5–7.

Lewicki, R. J., Bunker, B. B., 1995. "Trust in relationships: A model of development and decline," in B. B. Bunker, J. Z. Rubin & Associates (eds.), *Conflict, Cooperation and Justice: Essays Inspired by the Work of Morton Deutsch*. San Francisco, CA: Jossey-Bass Publishers, 133–173.

Light, I., 1972. *Ethnic Enterprise in America: Business and Welfare Among Chinese, Japanese and Blacks*, Berkeley: University of California Press.

Light, I., 1984. "Immigrants and ethnic enterprise in North America," *Ethnic and Racial Studies*, 7: 195–216.

Light, I., 2001. "Globalization, transnationalism and trade," *Asian and Pacific Migration Journal*, 10: 53–79.

Light, I., Bonacich, E., 1988. *Immigrant Entrepreneurs: Koreans in Los Angeles, 1965–1982*, Berkeley: University of California Press.

Light, I., Gold, S. J., 2000. *Ethnic Economies*, New York: Academic Press.

Luo, Y., 1997. "Partner selection and venturing success: The case of joint ventures with firms in the People's Republic of China," *Organizational Science*, 8: 648–662.

Luo, Y., Peng, M. W., 1999, "Learning to compete in a transition economy: Experience, environment, and performance," *Journal of International Business Studies*, 30: 269–296.

Madsen, T. K., Servais, P., 1997. "The internationalization of born globals: An evolutionary process," *International Business Review*, 6/6: 561–584.

Madsen, T. K., Rasmussen, E. S., Servais, P., 2000. "Differences and similarities between born globals and other types of exporters," in A. Yaprak & J. Tutek (eds.), *Globalization, The Multinational Firm, and Emerging Economies, (Advances in International Marketing*, 10), Amsterdam: JAI/Elsevier Inc., 247–265.

Mamis, R. A., 1989. "Global start-up," *Inc.*, Aug.: 38–47.

Manolova, T. 2003. "Small multinationals in global competition: An industry perspective," in H. Etemad & R. Wright (eds.), *Globalization and Entrepreneurship*, Cheltenham, UK: Edward Elgar, 59–81.

Marger, M. N., Hoffman, C. A., 1992. "Ethnic enterprise in Ontario: Immigrant participation in the small business sector," *International Migration Review*, 26:968–981.

Mars, G., Ward, R., 1984. "Ethnic business development in Britain: Opportunities and resources," in R. Ward, R. Jenkins (eds.), *Ethnic Communities in Business: Strategies for Economic Survival*, Cambridge: Cambridge University Press, 1–20.

Marschan-Piekkari, R., Welch, C., 2004. *Handbook of Qualitative Research Methods for International Business*, Cheltenham: Edward Elgar.

Marvasti, Amir B., 2004. *Qualitative Research in Sociology*, London: Sage.

Mayer, R. C., Davis, J. J., Schoorman, F. D., 1995. "An integrative model of organizational trust," *Academy of Management Review*, 20/3: 709–734.

McAllister, D. J., 1995. "Affect- and cognition-based trust as foundations for interpersonal cooperation in organizations," *Academy Management Journal*, 38/1: 24–59.

McAuley, A., 1999. "Entrepreneurial instant exporters in the Scottish arts and craft sector," *Journal of International Marketing*, 7: 67–82.

McClelland, D. A., 1961. *The Achieving Society*, Princeton, NJ: Van Nostrand.

McDougall, P. P., 1989. "International versus domestic entrepreneurship: new venture strategic behavior and industry structure," *Journal of Business Venturing*, 4: 387–400.

McDougall, P. P., Oviatt, B. M., 1996. "New venture internationalization, strategic change, and performance: A follow-up study," *Journal of Business Venturing*, 11/1: 23–40.

McDougall, P. P., Oviatt, B. M., 1997. "International entrepreneurship literature in the 1990s and directions for future research," in D. L. Sexton & R. W. Smilor (eds.), *Entrepreneurship 2000*, Chicago: Upstart Publishing, 291–320.

McDougall, P. P., Oviatt, B. M., 2000. "International entrepreneurship: The intersection of two paths," Guest Editor's Introduction, *Academy of Management Journal*, 43/5: 902–908.

McDougall, P. P., Oviatt, B. M., 2003. "Some fundamental issues in international entrepreneurship," http://www.hajarian.com/esterategic/tarjomeh/88-1/farahzadi.pdf.

McDougall, P. P., Shane, S., Oviatt, B. M., 1994. "Explaining the formation of international new ventures: The limits of theories from international business research," *Journal of Business Venturing*, 9/6: 469–487.

Michailova, S., 2000. "Contrasts in culture: Russian and western perspectives on organizational change," *The Academy of Management Executive*, 14/4: 99–112.

Michailova, S., Liuhto, K., 2000. "Organizational and management research in transition economies: Towards improved research methodologies," *Journal of East-West Business*, 6/3: 7–46.

Milliman, J., Von Glinow, M. A., 1998. "Research and publishing issues in large scale cross-national studies," *Journal of Managerial Psychology*, 13: 137–142.

Mitchell, R. K., Smith, J. B., Morse, E. A., Seawright, K. W., Peredo, A. M., McKenzie, B., 2002. "Are entrepreneurial cognitions universal? Assessing entrepreneurial cognitions across cultures," *Entrepreneurship, Theory and Practice*, 26/4: 9–32.

Mitchell, R. K., Smith, B., Seawright, K. W., Morse, E. A., 2000. "Cross-cultural cognitions and the venture creation decision," *Academy of Management Journal*, 43/5: 974–993.

Moen, Ø., 2000. "SMEs and international marketing: Investigating the differences in export strategy between firms of different size," *Journal of Global Marketing*, 13/4: 7–28.

Moen, Ø., Servais, P., 2002. "Born global or gradual global? Examining the export behaviour of small and medium-sized enterprises," *Journal of International Marketing*, 10/3: 49–72.

Morrow, J. F., 1988. "International entrepreneurship: A new growth opportunity," *New Management*, 3/5: 59–61.

Nahapiet, J., Ghoshal, S., 1998. "Social capital, intellectual capital, and the organizational advantage," *Academy of Management Review*, 23: 242–266.

Nakane, C., 1973. *Japanese Society*, New York: Penguin.

Nason, S., Pulillutla, M. M., 1998. "Towards a model of international research teams," *Journal of Managerial Psychology*, 13: 156–166.

Newsweek Staff, 2004. "E.T., phone home!" *Newsweek*, 9 May, http://www.newsweek.com/et-phone-home-127871.

OECD, 1997. *Globalization and Small and Medium Enterprises*, Paris: Organization for Economic Cooperation and Development.

Oviatt, B., McDougall, P., 1994. "Towards a theory of international new ventures," *Journal of International Business Studies*, 25/1: 45–64.

Oviatt, B. M., McDougall, P. P., 1995. "Global start-ups: Entrepreneurs on a worldwide stage," *Academy of Management Executive*, 9, 30–43.

Oviatt, B. M., McDougall, P. P., 1999. "A framework for understanding accelerated international entrepreneurship," in R. Wright (ed.), *Research in Global Strategic Management*, Stamford, CT: JAI Press, 23–40.

Oviatt, B., McDougall, P., 2000. "International entrepreneurship: The intersection of two research paths," *Academy of Management Journal*, 43: 902–908.

Peng, M., Luo, Y., 2000. "Managerial ties and firm performance in a transition economy: The nature of a micro-macro link," *Academy of Management Journal*, 43: 486–502.

Peng, M. W., 2001. "How entrepreneurs create wealth in transition economies," *Academy of Management Executive*, 15/1: 95–108.

Peteraf, M., Shanley, M., 1997. "Getting to know you: A theory of strategic group identity," *Strategic Management Journal*, 18 (summer special issue): 165–186.

Pickles, J., 2001. "There are no Turks in Bulgaria: Violence, ethnicity, and economic practice in the border regions and Muslim communities of post-Socialist Bulgaria," Mark Planck Institute for Social Anthropology Working Papers, Working Paper No: 25, Halle/Saale.

Pickles, J., Begg, R., 2000. "Ethnicity, state violence, and neo-liberal transitions in post-Communist Bulgaria," Special Issue of *Growth and Change: Ethnicity, Violence, and Regional Change*, 31/2: 179–210.

Portes, A., 1981. "Modes of structural incorporation and present theories of labor immigration," in M. Kritz, C. B. Keely, S. M. Tomasi (eds.), *Global Trends in Migration*. New York: Center for Migration Studies, 279–297.

Portes, A., 1989. "Contemporary immigration: Theoretical perspectives on its determinants and modes of incorporation," *International Migration Review*, 3: 606–630.

Portes, A., Jensen, L., 1989. "The enclave and the entrants: Patterns of ethnic enterprise in Miami before and after Mariel," *American Sociological Review*, 54: 929–949.

Pratt, M. L., 1992. *Imperial Eyes: Travel Writing and Transculturation*. London and New York: Routledge.

Punnet, B. J., Shenkar, O., 1994. "International Management Research," special double issue of *International Studies of Management and Organization*, 2.

Rabinow, P., 1986. "Representations are social facts: Modernity and post-modernity in anthropology," *Writing Culture*, J. Clifford & G. Marcus (eds.), London: University of California Press, 234–261.

Rasmussen, E. S., Madsen, T. K., & Evangelista, F., 2001. "The founding of the born global company in Denmark and Australia: Sensemaking and networking," *Asia Pacific Journal of Marketing and Logistics*, 13: 75–107.

Ray, D. M., 1989. "Strategic implications of entrepreneurial ventures 'born international': Four case studies," paper presented at the Frontiers in Entrepreneurship Research, Babson-Kauffman Entrepreneurship Research Conference.

Reed-Danahay, D., 1997. "Leaving home: Schooling stories and the ethnography of autoethnography in rural France," in D. Reed-Danahay (ed.), *Auto/Ethnography: Rewriting the Self and the Social*, Oxford and New York: Berg.

Rennie, M., 1993. "Global competitiveness: Born global," *McKinsey Quarterly*, 4: 45–52.

Rialp-Criado, A., Rialp-Criado, J., Knight, G. A., 2002. "The phenomenon of international new ventures, global start-ups, and born-globals: What do we know after a decade (1993–2002) of exhaustive scientific inquiry?" Working-paper no. 2002/11. Bellaterra (Barcelona), Spain: Dep. d'Economia de l'Empresa, Universitat Autònoma de Barcelona.

Roberts, E. B., Senturia, T. A., 1996. "Globalizing the emerging high-technology company," *Industrial Marketing Management*, 25: 491–506.

Rosen, M., 1988. "You asked for it: Christmas at the bosses' expense," *Journal of Management Studies*, 25/5: 463–480.

Rosen, M., 1991. "Coming to terms with the field: Understanding and doing organizational ethnography," *Journal of Management Studies*, 28/5: 1–24.

Rousseau, D. M., Sitkin, S. B., Burt, R. S., Camerer, C., 1998. "Not so different after all: A cross-discipline view of trust," *Academy of Management Review*, 23/3: 393–404.

Saxenian, A., 2000. "The origins and dynamics of production networks in Silicon Valley," in M. Kenney, (ed.), *Understanding Silicon Valley: The Anatomy of an Innovative Region*, Stanford, CA: Stanford University Press.

Sharma, D. D., Blomstermo, A., 2003. "The internationalization process of born globals," *International Business Review*, 12/6: 739–754.

Shenkar, O., von Glinow, M. A., 1994, "Paradoxes of organizational theory and research: Using the case of China to illustrate national contingency," *Management Science*, 40: 56–71.

Silverman, D., 1993. *Interpreting Qualitative Data*, Thousand Oaks, CA: Sage.

Silverman, D., 1985. *Qualitative Methodology & Sociology*, Brookfield, VT: Gower.

Simmel, G., 1950. *The Sociology of Georg Simmel*, Free Press.

Simões, V. C.Dominguinhos, P. M., 2001. "Portuguese born globals: An exploratory study," paper presented at the 27th EIBA Conference, Paris, France.

Smith, K. G., Gannon, M. J., Sapienza, H. J., 1989. "Selecting methodologies for entrepreneurial research: Trade-offs and guidelines," *Entrepreneurship: Theory & Practice*, 14/1: 39–49.

Snell, R., Easterby-Smith, M., 1991. "Peeking through the bamboo curtain," in N. Campbell, D. Brown (eds.), *Advances in Chinese Industrial Studies*, Vol. 2, *The Changing Nature of Management in China*, London: JAI Press, 163–170.

Sowell, T., 1996. *Migration and Cultures: A World View*, New York: Basic Books.

Sparkes, A. C., 2000. "Autoethnography and narratives of self: Reflections on criteria in action," *Sociology of Sport Journal*, 17: 21–41.

Starr, J. E., MacMillan, I. C., 1990. "Resource cooptation via social contracting: Resource acquisition strategies for new ventures," *Strategic Management Journal*, 11/1: 79–92.

Steers, R. M., Bischoff, S. J., Higgins, L. H., 1992. "Cross-cultural management research: The fish and the fishermen," *Journal of Management Inquiry*, 1: 321–330.

Teagarden, M. B., Von Glinow, M. A., Bowen, D. E., Frayne, C. A., Nason, S., Huo, Y. P., Milliman, J., Arias, M. E., Butler, M. C., Geringer, J. M.,

Kim, N. M., Scullion, H., Lowe, K. B., Drost, E. A., 1995. "Toward a theory of comparative management research: An idiographic case study of the best international human resources management project," *Academy of Management Journal*, 38: 1261–1287.

Timmons, J. A., 1994. *New Venture Creation: Entrepreneurship for the 21st Century*. Fourth edition. Burr Ridge, IL: Irwin Press.

Tsang, E., 2001. "Internationalizing the family firm: A case study of a Chinese family firm," *Journal of Small Business Management*, 39/1: 88–94.

Turati, C., Usai, A., Ravagnani, R., 1998. "Antecedents of co-ordination in academic project research," *Journal of Managerial Psychology*, 13: 188–198.

United Nations Conference on Trade and Development (UNCTAD), 2001. "World investment report," New York: UNCTAD.

United Nations Conference on Trade and Development (UNCTAD), 2002. "World investment report 2002: Transnational corporations and export performance," New York and Geneva: United Nations.

Usunier, Jean-Claude, 1998. *International and cross-cultural management research*, London: Sage.

Van Maanen, J., 1979a. "The fact of fiction in organizational ethnography," *Administrative Science Quarterly*, 24/4: 539–550.

Van Maanen, J., 1979b. "Reclaiming qualitative methods for organizational research: A preface," *Administrative Science Quarterly*, 24: 520–524.

Van Maanen, J., 1995. *Representations in Ethnography*, Sage Publications.

Van de Ven, A. H., Poole, M. S., 1990. "Methods for studying innovation development in the Minnesota Innovation Research Program," *Organization Science*, 1/3: 313–334.

Vernon, R., 1966. "International investment and international trade in the product cycle," *Quarterly Journal of Economics*, 80: 190–207.

Waldinger, R., 1986. "Immigrant enterprise: A critique and reformulation," *Theory and Society*, 15:249–285.

Waldinger, R., Aldrich, H., Ward, R., 1990. *Ethnic Entrepreneurs: Immigrant Business in Industrial Societies*, Thousand Oaks, CA: Sage.

Welch, C., Marschan-Piekkari, R., 2004. "Qualitative Research in International Business: State of the Art," in R. Marschan-Piekkari & R. Welch (eds.), *Handbook of Qualitative Research Methods for International Business*, Cheltenham: Edward Elgar: 5–24.

Wellman, D., 1994. "Constructing ethnographic authority: The work process of field research and ethnographic account," *Cultural Studies*, 8/3: 569–583.

Williamson, O. E., 1975. *Markets and Hierarchies: Analysis and Antitrust Implications*, New York: Free Press.

Wilson, K., Martin, W. A., 1982. "Ethnic enclaves: A comparison of Cuban and black economies in Miami," *American Journal of Sociology*, 88: 135–160.

Wilson, K., Portes, A., 1980. "Immigrant enclaves: An analysis of the labor market experience of Cubans in Miami," *American Journal of Sociology*, 86: 259–319.

Wong, L., 1997. "Globalization and transnational migration: A study of recent Chinese capitalist immigration from the Asia Pacific to Canada," *International Sociology,* 12: 329–351.

Yin, R. K., 1994 / 2003. *Case study research: Design and Methods,* Thousand Oaks, CA: Sage Publications.

Yukseker, D., 2003. *Laleli-Moskova Mekiği: Kayıtdışı Ticaret ve Cinsiyet İlişkileri* [*The Laleli-Moscow Shuttle: Informal Trade and Gender Relations*], İstanbul: İletişim Yayınları.

Zaheer, S., 1995. "Overcoming the liability of foreignness," *Academy of Management Journal,* 38: 341–363.

Zahra, S., 2005. "A theory of international new ventures: A decade of research," *Journal of International Business Studies,* 36, 20–28.

Zahra, S., Bogner, A. W. C., 2000. "Technology strategy and software new ventures' performance: Exploring the moderating effect of the competitive environment," *Journal of Business Venturing,* 15: 135–173.

Zahra, S., Garvis, D., 2000. "International corporate entrepreneurship and firm performance: The moderating effect of international environmental hostility," *Journal of Business Venturing,* 15/4: 469–492.

Zahra, S. A., George, G., 2002. "International entrepreneurship: The current status of the field and future research agenda," in M. A. Hitt, R. D. Ireland, S. M. Camp, & D. L. Sexton (eds.), *Strategic Entrepreneurship: Creating a New Mindset,* Oxford: Blackwell Publishers.

Zahra, S. A., Ireland, D. R., Hitt, M. A., 2000. "International expansion by new venture firms: International diversity, mode of market entry, technological learning and performance," *Academy of Management Journal,* 43/5: 925–950.

Zahra, S., Neubaum, D., Huse, M., 1996. "The effect of the environment on the firm's export intensity," *Entrepreneurship: Theory & Practice,* 22/1: 25–46.

Zahra, S., Nielsen, A.Bogner, W., 1999. "Corporate entrepreneurship, knowledge and competence development," *Entrepreneurship: Theory & Practice,* 23/3: 169–189.

Zahra, S., Schulte, W., 1994. "International entrepreneurship: Beyond folklore and myth," *International Journal of Commerce and Management,* 4/1–2: 85–95.

Zimmer, C., Aldrich, H. E., 1987. "Resource mobilization through ethnic networks: Kinship and friendship ties of shopkeepers in England," *Sociological Perspectives,* 30: 422–445.

Index

Page numbers in italics refer to figures. Page numbers in bold refer to tables.

Printed in the United States
by Baker & Taylor Publisher Services